"Joy often feels like a fickle and elusive [?] the challenges of raising a child with sp[?], Laurie Wallin takes parents like you and me by the hand. In the telling of her story, we learn that she once lost her joy and then, by the grace of God, found it again. Then she gently guides us back to the joy waiting to be found and embraced when we choose forgiveness and gratitude instead of blame and bitterness. If you need to get your joy back—and what parent of a child with special needs doesn't at some point in life?— Laurie Wallin's encouraging book is the place to make it happen."

—Jolene Philo, author of *Different Dream Parenting*

"When I fly with my boys, the flight attendant stops by our row and reminds me that if there's an emergency, I'm supposed to put on my oxygen mask before I help the boys put on theirs. Laurie's words remind me of that principle—if I'm not taking care of myself, I can't take care of anyone else. Writing honestly about her own struggles and successes, Laurie guides readers through areas of unforgiveness that, if left unchecked, can become areas of bitterness. She will be your biggest cheerleader as she helps you examine your heart and release what's holding you back from experiencing joy."

—Sandra Peoples, coauthor of *Held: Learning to Live in God's Grip*

"As a special needs parent I have lived in that isolated, lonely, and broken place for many years. Laurie bravely pulls back the curtain on the struggles and emotions that come with having a special needs child. But she doesn't stop there. She grabs you by the hand and walks with you from that broken place to a place where you can live life with joy and contentment. A place where you can enjoy motherhood and your children."

—LaToya Edwards, author of *Beautifully Broken*

"The world needs this book. I need this book. *Get Your Joy Back* is a communion from which all special needs parents should partake. Read it and expect to be validated, encouraged, challenged, and spurred on."

—Gillian Marchenko, author of *Sun Shine Down: A Memoir*

"Laurie writes while in the trenches—her words mixed with humor and reality will resonate with parents as we battle resentment and fight for joy in the world of special needs. This book will ask you to shift your gaze by the power of forgiveness and lead you to cultivate joy in the deep parts of your heart and in every relationship. By the end, you will realize you're no longer staring at a dark wall but have a choice to enter a grace-filled place with breathtaking possibility, hope, and joy."

—Kara Dedert, blogger at karadedert.com

Get Your Joy Back

Banishing Resentment and Reclaiming Confidence in
Your Special Needs Family

LAURIE WALLIN

Kregel
Publications

To my mom, Beverly,
who prayed me through this project.
And to my husband and daughters,
for courageously permitting me to share our story.

CONTENTS

Foreword

Bob and Stephanie sat in the parking lot, watching as people entered the church for Sunday services. Julie, their teenage daughter, sat in the back seat with Jason, their 10-year-old son with autism. "Why are we just sitting here?" Julie fumed. "Why aren't we going in?"

Stephanie glanced at her husband, wondering the same thing. Bob's jaw was taut and his eyes were damp. Right then Jason began his usual rocking back and forth and hitting his legs. "Help your brother!" Bob barked at Julie. As she grabbed Jason's arm, Stephanie reached for her husband's hand and whispered, "If you want to skip this, we can."

The family was new to this church. Bob had explained to the pastor that Jason had autism and would need assistance in the children's class. The first few Sundays had passed without any disruption, but last week was different. The children's class became noisy, which created "sensory overload" for Jason—he went ballistic, frightening his classmates and alarming his teacher.

Bob and Stephanie were told that Jason could not attend Sunday school anymore without adult supervision. They left church that day feeling guilty and embarrassed.

Bob broke the silence. "So which one of us should sit out here with Jason? You or me?" he asked, glancing at Stephanie. They could hear the service getting started with singing. Bob looked at his watch. "Maybe we'll come back next week," he abruptly announced and started the engine.

"Aw, man," Julie whined. "I was just beginning to make friends here." The family drove away in stony silence.

The story is true. And it's repeated countless times every day—maybe not in a church parking lot, but in restaurants, shopping malls, and supermarkets everywhere. Mothers and fathers of kids with special needs are in desperate need of help. And the fact that you are reading this book indicates that you are probably one of those mothers or fathers. You've poured out your heart in support groups, you've gone on websites to gather info on your child's disability, but still, your energy is sapped and your joy is drained.

You love your child. You'd give anything to lighten his or her load; still, you find yourself looking back on your wedding day, wondering if you'd have said your vow had you known what you were getting into. Disability can test the best of marriages. And if you're a single parent raising a child with special needs? It's doubly hard.

This is why I give a hearty thumbs-up for Laurie Wallin and the insights she shares in *Get Your Joy Back: Banishing Resentment and Reclaiming Confidence in Your Special Needs Family*. Laurie understands the pitfalls (but also the incredible joys) of keeping your family's sanity when disability is in the mix. She speaks from great experience, so I encourage you to turn each page slowly—savor the insights and write down the suggestions; use a yellow highlighter and reflect often on the illustrations. Start a journal and write down personal and family goals. Gain as much wisdom as you can and know that you are not . . . alone.

You are part of a growing movement of parents of children with disabilities who are heaven-bent on trusting God in all the hard places of your family's life. You are among those who understand that, yes, life is supposed to be difficult—but it opens the way for God to pour out grace upon grace into your weakness. Most of all, you are among that remarkable echelon of parents who cling tenaciously to hope. Just like my friends Bob and Stephanie who, by the way, are beginning to make big strides forward in their family.

So be encouraged, friend. Help is on the way—and it begins as you start turning the pages of *Get Your Joy Back*.

Joni Eareckson Tada
Joni and Friends International
Disability Center
Agoura Hills, California

Invitation

COME IN FROM THE COLD

"Hold on a second," I tell my friend on the phone. "I can barely hear you. Let me see if I can get a better signal." I walk to the next room in my house. The kids are all in there, drawing, playing games—doing the kinds of things that will inevitably pull me from my phone call within the next three minutes—when two of the four girls start arguing over whose marker is whose.

"Okay, I hear you now," I say. But as she talks, I hear her voice in broken fragments. So I move again. "Hang on, let me try another room," I say loudly, as though my volume change will overcome the lack of connection. In the back of my mind, the timer is ticking—the one that keeps me vigilant with my daughter who has enuresis and encopresis (chronic wetting and soiling conditions). *How long since she's gone to the bathroom?* I wonder, then dismiss the thought as I walk and check with my friend: "Can you hear me now?"

No dice.

I walk outside my house, stand on the driveway, and try again. "What about now?"

Nope.

I keep walking and checking in with her, until I find the perfect signal. Crystal clear, I hear her talking about a situation at work, about her family, and how she's doing. We talk for about twenty minutes and say our goodbyes. I'm in shock as I realize I snuck in a whole conversation without . . .

The screaming.

How long has that been going on? I groan.

I begin to stand up and realize I've been sitting on the concrete in the corner of my driveway, feet in the street. Muscles stiff, arm tired from holding the phone in chilly evening air, I stand up and stretch. Half stumbling, I will my body toward the too-common battlefield inside. *How did I not notice I was cold, uncomfortable, and stiff until now?* Because that's what we parents do. We accommodate. We manage situations, life, our kids, their needs, our marriages, and whatever else is happening—most of the time not even knowing how we're doing in the moment or what we might need—until our bodies, minds, or best friends tell us we're a mess. That's the crisis point that reminds us we've been sitting in the cold for God knows how long, trying to get a signal in that situation or relationship.

Welcome to the book that will help stop the madness. A resource that will equip you to stop ignoring yourself and pushing a hundred miles past what you can reasonably give as you care for kids who are extra . . . everything. A little (or a lot of) extra energy, effort, emotion, care, planning, and discipline. While dozens of wonderful, practical books exist for us who raise children with all combinations of special needs, this one is dedicated solely to you and your well-being.

A well-being that includes and extends beyond the physical, emotional, mental, and social realms of existence. That allows you to daily say it is well with your soul in all of the relationships you encounter as a parent, many of which can seem to be more of a stressor than a blessing when you're raising kids who are . . . *special.* Kids outside the bell curve: possibly clinically diagnosed with one or more special needs, or maybe "just" an overflowing handful of strong-willed, toddler-aged, or extra-smart personhood.

If the child you're raising is clinically diagnosed with a special need (or, like ours, a few each), or you suspect they've got one, or your child isn't even technically a child anymore (they're over eighteen) and your friends are off on cruises and you're still walking your grown man-child to therapist appointments, this book is for you.

You, that parent who needs to take care of yourself in the lifelong ministry that is raising your special child. You, the person who serves as a buffer when your child's reality clashes with the school's, their friend's, their doctor's, or the unsuspecting passerby at the store. You, the person who is more than simply "parent," who has unexplored or underdeveloped gifts and talents God wants you to recognize, use, and enjoy abundantly. You, the one who's been sitting on the far corner of your cold concrete driveway, neglecting yourself for way too long. You, whom God desires to live deep, life-giving joy today—and every day—into eternity.

God desires you to live deep,
life-giving joy today—and
every day—into eternity.

Sound too good to be true? Yeah, I hear that a lot. At a conference I attended recently, a mom of a child with bipolar disorder shared her story, heard mine, hugged me, and pulled back incredulously, asking, "With your family situation, how is it that you're smiling, dressed in matching clothes, and have your hair and makeup done?" Not that looking put together means I'm internally put together, but it does say something: taking care of ourselves isn't the norm as parents raising kids with extra needs. It's the exception. But it's also *possible*—and even graspable—if we get intentional, get realistic, and get rid of what holds us back more than anything else: the stress.

That's what I hope this book will do for you—help you deal with your stress in ways that are intentional, realistic, and that make space for the joy you sorely need. Not happiness-joy, or feelings-joy (though those are good too), but "the joy of the Lord is our strength" kind of joy. Joy that bolsters you against challenges. Joy that replenishes the depleted hopes and dreams. Joy that restores you after those days you think you'll never get through. Joy that whispers "you matter" when you feel invisible, that shouts "God reigns" when you've started to lose hope for that long-awaited treatment. Joy that fills the empty moments and overflows into the lives of others, with extra to spare.

Ready for that kind of joy? Then read on, brave friend!

Laurie

One

YES, YOU *CAN* ENJOY LIFE AGAIN

"I'm so tired," she says, looking down at the table, her finger tracing the wood's grain. "I just don't know what to do."

I nod. I know that place too.

"I mean, my daughter's so intense. I've read every book and article that's supposed to help. I've tried everything people recommend. All that work with counselors led us nowhere. The classes, support groups . . . even getting her an IEP . . ." Her voice trails off. She's looking for something. Words? Feelings? Maybe the magic bullet she's missed that would make everything just . . . work. Or make any sense whatsoever.

"And you know what? I even tried that crazy idea from the tabloid magazine!" She laughs. But her eyes search mine for judgment.

"See?" I seize her levity. "You're as nuts as I said you were!"

She laughs again. I smile too. Then tears fall. Fast.

"We're doing the best we can with our daughter," she continues. "I just don't have a clue how I'm going to do this forever! I can't even relax sitting here at lunch with a friend."

Tears keep coming. I hold her hand and we sit together. I want to embrace and hold her tight. Make her laugh again. Tell her she's not alone. But she may as well be on an island at the South Pole right now. Even sitting with someone who understands as I do—even amidst the smiles, the touch, the gallows humor—the isolation she feels is almost palpable.

What about you? How are *you* holding up?

If you're like me, the answer is probably something like, "What do you mean . . . 'me'?" And if that's how you're feeling, I assure you, you are not alone.

I repeat: you are not alone.

There's not much space in a family with special needs kids for us as parents to have a life of our own. Or even consider one. Instead, we manage our longings and stress in odd ways. Maybe you can relate to my experience a few years ago.

With one child diagnosed and beginning medications, hope was rekindled for life without hours-long screaming fits and broken walls. But then, after years of appointments, when our second daughter's moods still raged undeterred, I stuffed the stress deep inside. I ate it away. I cried it away. I took antidepressants. I blogged it away. I overextended-myself-in-service'd it away. I screamed it away. I even punched-a-hole-in-my-bedroom-wall'd it away.

It didn't go away.

All I was left with was a chubby, angry, bitter, overworked me . . . and a hole (or two) to patch in my wall. I looked in the mirror one morning and said, "Lady, you look *old*." At thirty-five!

Turns out there's a reason for that. (Here's where I geek-out on you. I used to be a science teacher.) Aging happens as our DNA, the delicate molecular template for life in all our cells, begins to unravel. We all have special structures called telomeres that cap the ends of our DNA strands, stunting the aging (unraveling) process. Unfortunately, stress causes these protective caps to shrink and wear out. In other words, we are actually aging faster than we would have without the chronic, unrelenting pressures of caregiving.

Great news, right?

In a recent documentary, UCSF researcher Dr. Elizabeth Blackburn reported that the length (and thus protective nature) of telomeres is much shorter for parents in our situation. Stanford University neurobiologist Robert Sapolsky added that for every year of chronological age, special needs moms experienced roughly six years of cellular aging.[1]

My friend at lunch that day is not the only tired, stressed-out parent raising special needs kids. We're all living it. We get up, wash up, make the coffee, and jump in with both feet to intense lives of:

Repetitive, rigorous physical care. We lift, shift, bathe, and assist our kids. In cases like my daughters', who have mood and developmental disabilities, we must even restrain them and physically protect siblings when they act out aggressively.

Hyper-vigilance. We maintain for a lifetime the level of vigilance most parents need only while their kids are infants and toddlers. We constantly consider and balance diverging opinions of professionals, family, and friends about how our children should develop or respond.

Intense emotion. We experience loss daily (whether or not we realize it)[2] and continuously cycle through grief. We do this throughout our entire parenting journey as our kids struggle, suffer, miss milestones, hit milestones (two decades late), or get rejected. In the meantime we have a life mismatched with what we had hoped for ourselves as parents.

Isolation. It's a tiring job to be caregivers as well as educators of all who interact with our families and our children. Sometimes we're isolated due to the nature of our children's special needs. Or we opt for isolation instead of having to explain ourselves—again—to someone who doesn't understand.

Fears about the future. For some of us, it's a very real possibility that our kids will die before we will. Or that they'll need a high level of care even as adults or after we pass on. We worry about how transitions in living arrangements will transpire, and fear how their care will weigh on our other children or extended family members.

Chronic stress unravels us. It agitates us and messes with our weight, sleep, memory, energy level, and long-term moods. It blanches our view of life, ourselves, our marriages, and our kids. Then again, I don't have to tell you that. You're already living it.

As a mom of four—the older two foster-adopted who, between the two of them, boast diagnoses of bipolar disorder, anxiety, ODD, ADHD, seizures, enuresis, encopresis, sensory integration problems, and speech and developmental delays—I've struggled hard and often with feeling numb and resentful. I've been angry over what I've lost: the family I imagined, the kids I'd dreamed about, the life where I didn't have to do damage control with onlookers as my twelve-year-old goes ballistic in the middle of a supermarket parking lot. I've longed for the alternate universe where I don't constantly struggle with feeling guilty, inept, lonely, and depressed, especially when I consider what life is like for my two younger children, who are growing up in a family with an intensity they never asked for.

The point here is not to add to your stress . . . or to languish in mine. It's to recognize how real and intense our daily stressors can be, and how crucial it is to our health and well-being to learn to thrive despite them all. To do that will take something a lot stronger than we can muster through positive attitude, coping strategies, and punching the eighty-pound bag at the gym (although all of these do help!). No, it will take something much more powerful. Something supernatural, infinitely bigger than ourselves and the problems we and our kids face.

> The point here is not to add to your stress . . . or to languish in mine. It's to recognize how real and intense our daily stressors can be, and how crucial it is to our health and well-being to learn to thrive despite them all.

THE SECRET TO DISSOLVING OUR STRESS

At the end of my rope five years ago, I got invited to a seminar on forgiveness at a retreat. "Oh good," I groaned to myself. "Another super-spiritual topic that won't relate to my daily life." I did not want to go, but my good friend was teaching it—the friend who's prayed with me through fifteen years of ups and downs. So I sucked it up and went.

An hour later, I left the session feeling good that I'd supported my friend, but feeling even more angry at the process of forgiveness. Not because the talk was preachy or negative. She'd shared some of her own journey with forgiveness, and how she'd seen it follow three steps: (1) note the hurt, (2) choose to let it go, and (3) move on with life. She'd emphasized her own struggle with facing the truth that God requires us to forgive—even the hardest, most painful hurts—because we've been forgiven so much. All of it was familiar theology. Nothing earth-shattering or hard to understand. So, why were my fists clenched and hot tears streaming down my cheeks? Probably because the whole time I was thinking, "I'm sure this tidy little three-step model works just fine when someone cuts me off on the freeway. It really breaks down when I have frustrations, anger, and wrongs coming at me every day." As my friend shared her presentation, my mind wandered to scenarios: if I were to forgive like this—acknowledging a hurt and choosing forgiveness each time my challenging kids give way to their darker sides, or a well-meaning friend recommends a basic parenting book to "solve" my parenting problems, or a doctor invalidates all the consistent work I've been doing with my girls—I'd be forgiving all day long. I'd never be able to think about another topic again!

"Just go ahead and end it here, Lord!" I whined.

He didn't.

After that seminar, I finally felt the stress. Really felt it. Everything and everyone seemed totally unmanageable—a ton of bricks piled on top of me right where I sat. I'd prayed, confessed my own shortcomings, memorized Scripture, and chanted "I forgive [fill in offending person's name here]." It wasn't getting any easier to forgive. I felt desperate and distracted. My breath short, I felt anger and despair pressing in on me. I finally saw how I'd been pushing people away—it was simply too much work to build relationships when they often brought so much hurt, and my kids already needed 97 percent of my focus and energy.

I tried to ignore the turmoil caused by knowing God wanted me to forgive, and feeling like that was just one more item on an already overwhelming list of you'll-never-get-these-done tasks. Over and over, like a punch in the gut, the forgiveness idea kept resurfacing. In conversations, in books I read, in devotionals on which I reflected. Clearly I was missing something. But what?

Then, in one of the books, I came across this quote from Anne Lamott: "There [are] admonitions [everywhere] about the self-destructiveness of not forgiving people, and reminders that this usually doesn't hurt other people so much as it hurts you. In fact, not forgiving is like drinking rat poison and then waiting for the rat to die."[3]

Light flooded my mind. I saw it: my life was hard with special needs kids, the stress was killing me, and it was in large part because of *me*. I resented (withheld forgiveness from) just about everyone in my life instead of connecting meaningfully with them. I'd been living the emotional and—even though my high cholesterol hadn't been diagnosed yet— physical reality of Deepak Chopra's metaphor for resentment: "Holding on to resentment is like holding on to your breath. You'll soon start to suffocate."[4]

THE CHOICE TO TRULY LIVE AGAIN

At that point I had two choices: crumple under the weariness, hurt, and broken expectations, or learn how to forgive—release—others and myself to make space for something better. Something like a life again.

You have that choice too.

This book will help. It comes from my own (flawed!) journey to heal by spitting out the rat poison. By coming to understand forgiveness as an intentional way of life instead of another task to be done—forgiveness that acts like a filter in the midst of the ignorant comments of others, the disregarding tone of professionals, or my kids' ongoing behavioral challenges. Forgiveness as an act of surrender that opens the door for emotional relief and divine help in every aspect of life.

This book also comes from another part of me: the certified life coach who wants to see you—to see all of us—get unstuck and enjoy life again. To support you in living the invitation of Hebrews 12:1: "Since we are surrounded by such a great cloud of witnesses, let us throw off everything that hinders and the sin that so easily entangles. And let us run with perseverance the race marked out for us." Don't you love that imagery? The idea that we aren't confined to miserably carry the weights in our lives, or to crawl our way through the challenges we face? That we're invited to live for real—abundantly, with joy—to run with abandon together in freedom, no matter what we face?

And finally, this book comes from the experience of over seventy families who courageously shared their stories, struggles, and strengths in the online and phone surveys I conducted for this project. All our stories combine here to guide you as you discover what God can do when you choose forgiveness and healthy grief, and how these choices can change a family struggling with high needs kids into a family that thrives. They join the stories of hope from Scripture shared throughout this book to become that "great cloud of witnesses" who can spur you on in throwing off the stress weight that holds you down, to help you run with joy the unique race of life set before you.

Please allow these stories to come alongside and give you hope. Don't feel pressured to read from cover to cover all at once, but visit the sections that support you in the areas of greatest need right now. For me, the greatest need is often how I feel about God and His role in life's challenges. If that's you today too, go ahead and skip everything to go to chapters 14 and 15 and begin there. You can't do this book "right" or "wrong." It is one hundred percent here to support you as you lay aside the life weights that would hold you back from running with joy and abandon.

I pray that you'll give freedom a chance.

Two

LOOKING IN THE MIRROR (FORGIVING YOURSELF)

"My mind is a bad neighborhood I try not to go into alone."
—Anne Lamott

When I sent out the survey to ask parents which part of parenting kids with special needs was hardest, I think I was deep down hoping most of them would reveal it to be the struggle *within themselves*. I didn't realize I was looking for that at first, but when the results poured in, and I read through the seventy-plus responses, I began to ache inside.

So few checked that box. Only a handful acknowledged that they're struggling with how they feel about themselves as parents, how they see themselves in the mirror. Only a handful admitted that they question every move they make or don't make, or that they withdraw from relationship because they—if they got really honest for a moment—feel as though they're failing as moms, as dads . . . as human beings.

I actually put down this manuscript and walked away from it for a month because of the revelation of that moment. Maybe because I suddenly faced my worst fear: maybe I really *am* a bad parent. Maybe they know more than I do. Maybe those other parents have actually figured it out; maybe they haven't gained weight, gone gray, uttered swear words, picked up one-too-many glasses of wine, punched a wall, cried in their closet, or gone on antidepressants. Then I came across a blog post that revealed the truth.

HIDING BEHIND THE "EVERYTHING'S OKAY" FAÇADE

Gillian Marchenko, mother of two daughters with Down syndrome, wrote this on her blog:

> When dealing with our children with special needs, or kids in general, I don't think that we parents feel like we can really open up about our struggles. Good parents aren't supposed to struggle. Parents of kids who have special needs are supposed to grow instant thick skin, have endurance, and be ready to fight to the end for our kids. We're supposed to handle biting, slapping, outbursts, embarrassing situations, stares, rejection, with an easy, winning smile, and grace.[1]

First, did you catch that little "or kids in general" clause? Feeling like we can't open up about our struggles isn't unique to us with high-needs kids. Many parents, no matter what issues or non-issues our children have, struggle with comparing our messy twenty-four-hour-a-day lives with the polished snapshot versions we see in other families at church or community events. Humans have been comparing themselves to others and feeling like they come up short since the beginning of time (see Sarai and Hagar in Genesis 16, or Rachel and Leah in Genesis 29–30).

In this era, social media has allowed us to not only compare our lives to those of in-person family and neighbors, but to just about everyone on the planet. Researchers at the University of Michigan revealed that on Facebook, as an example, study participants experienced greater declines in moment-to-moment feelings of well-being and general life satisfaction following time spent on Facebook than they did in their in-person interactions.[2] A study of young adults in Utah found that the more time people spent on Facebook, the more they felt others were happier than them and that life was not fair.[3] Comparison does that to people—makes us feel less than, not good enough, insignificant. Add the insecurity and self-doubt we live as parents faced with impossible challenges like those in Marchenko's list, and is it any wonder we hide our exhausted, messy selves behind an irrational façade?

We'll keep up that charade for years, which is probably why few in the survey up to that point said they were upset with themselves as parents. Because who has an intact self after all that pretending? I don't. I'll admit it. There are days I wake up and look at myself in the mirror and don't even know who I am. Not that I don't know my name or the basic surface facts about my life, but that I don't personally know *me* anymore. What I love, what I want in life, my hopes, dreams, desires, frustrations. There's just this woman looking back at me, older than she should be, and I wonder "Who's that?" It's the same woman who, when asked by her husband how she's doing, takes so long to formulate an answer that she ends up skirting the question and talking about something else.

HIDING BEHIND THE TRY-TOO-HARD LIFE

We hide because even while we'd rarely admit it, we think the lives of our families hinge on us. And here I'm going to talk straight to the moms reading this. Women, we in particular, whether we like it or not, go into motherhood assuming some version of "if I do it right, my family will be happy and healthy." "Doing it right" entails lots of things:

if I pray enough
if I pray the right things
if I take my kids to the right specialists
if I spend enough time with them
if I use the right techniques to care for them
if I get the family on the same page in terms of their care (which, of
    course, includes expecting my husband to parent in exactly the
    way the therapist, doctor, or any other professional, author,
    teacher, . . . or whoever else specifies)
if I smile at church
if I tell my friends *just enough* of the struggle to be "real" . . . but not
    enough that they're overwhelmed by my situation and start to
    stare off into space

There are probably a thousand other things we could add to the list. It all boils down to this: we are *trying* instead of *being*. And this erases us. One mom from the survey, Michelle, admits: "It is stressful because I place more than due amount of emotional stress [and] complications on myself . . . [compounding the expectations that] already exist [and] making it even more challenging to maintain the joy I have." Why all this trying hard? From experience and conversations with parents, it's so we can be above reproach in how we manage our child's care and needs. Which earns us what? The right to parent? Significance in our peer circles? An award for passing muster in a world where people see children's health, behavior, and temperaments as solely caused (not just shaped) by parents? We've all fallen prey to these kinds of thoughts, friends. And not a single one is going to help us thrive as parents of our special kids.

It all boils down to this:
we are *trying* instead of *being*.
And this erases us.

Beyond the assumption that our families hinge on us, we try too hard because we equate trying with *loving* our kids. One mom, Anna, commented on Marchenko's post that "sometimes I feel like I have to put up this front that everything is wonderful and I have everything together because if I complain or seem stressed, then it might appear to others that I do not love my little girl with [Down syndrome]." How did we get to a place where our love for our kids must be validated by someone outside us, our child, and God? Again, we all "go there" as parents, but when we really step back, the absurdity of what keeps us spinning our wheels at two hundred miles-per-emotional-hour becomes much more clear! If we allow ourselves to fall into the try-too-hard trap for the sake of not seeming unloving as parents, there won't be any medals at the end of that journey. All there will be is resentment and emotional suffocation.

HIDING BEHIND BROKEN CHOICES

Marchenko, whom I mentioned earlier in the chapter, is the blessed soul who made me face this in my own life. In her poignant memoir *Sun Shine Down* she shares the deep darkness into which she plummeted after her daughter's birth and diagnosis with Down syndrome. In chapters that clutched my heart in stunned, nearly not breathing "You really get it!" tearfulness, she admits:

> I wanted to tell [my friend] I was afraid of my child and, in fact, I was now afraid of my life. I could not stop drinking because I would have to try to love [my daughter] on my own, without a manufactured glow of happiness to pull me towards her. Without alcohol, I couldn't take her in my arms and claim that gooey, newborn love—the wonder of a new baby . . . the stuff that a new mom should feel. The stuff I was void of.[4]

Nobody else I knew had shared before about the lengths to which we'll go in order to keep hiding from the grief—nobody until I found this book, this author. Her struggle is one I've faced too. It's that beyond-all-coping-skills pain that comes from realizing that we're raising a child who may never be okay. One who, like my second daughter, baffles every specialist in every field we pursue in our efforts to help her. One whose future sometimes seems as fathomless as the inside of a dark closet, complete with feelings of claustrophobic panic.

When the depression phase of grief hits like that, we can turn to anything, desperate to get away from the pain. We use food, alcohol, prescription drugs, sleeping, hours—or days—of TV, reading novels, surfing the internet . . . and the list goes on (we're really quite creative, aren't we?). We may even struggle with sexual sin, which is often in women a signal of stress or of feeling disconnected or undervalued[5]—two attributes for which moms of kids with special needs seem to me to have cornered the market.

The worst part about these ways we cope? They increase the maddening isolation from which we're already suffering as they send us down a road of "I shouldn't be doing this (or doing it for as long as I am)," which easily devolves into, "Who would understand or want to be in the life of someone so messed up?" And just like that, the enemy of our lives, who prowls the earth "like a roaring lion looking for someone to devour," pulls us away from the joy-giving support that we so urgently need (see 1 Peter 5:8).

HIDING BEHIND GOOD THINGS

While we can struggle with these kinds of hidden, seemingly shameful behaviors, our chronic grief and disappointment in ourselves can come out in other ways as well. Ways that are more socially acceptable . . . or even expected. Mine? It's cleaning the house. Recently I asked each of my kids how they view our family. One of my questions was, "What does Mom love to do?" I was hoping my kids would respond with "play with me," "take vacations," or "write." Becca, my tell-it-like-it-is kid, answered this way instead: "You like to randomly clean the house."

I laughed when she said it (the kid delivers wit with her wallop!). But I was crying inside because she thinks I love to clean my house. Like, more than anything else in the whole wide world, this is my dream. Why? Because I do it a lot. When I'm upset I clean and organize my kitchen counter, the space I use most in my house. When my second daughter has another wetting or soiling accident, I sweep the floor (because, after having to clean or oversee her cleaning it up, that piece of stray rice stuck to my foot might just throw me over the edge). When my oldest lurches into a heavily downward spiral in terms of her moods, I fold laundry. As much as I wanted to argue with my seven-year-old and her response, she'd gotten it right. I do love to clean the house—it's easier to clean a counter than engage with mental illness or Reactive Attachment Disorder.

Maybe you're a house cleaner, or maybe you cope with grief via just a little too much of some other socially acceptable behavior: running mile after mile, controlling your food intake, helping people until you're burned out—you name it. I've done all of those at some point. Eventually I blew out my knees, gave up on food control and gained twenty pounds, and withdrew from helping at the school. There's only so much trying hard that we can do before we're toast, right?

Why am I harping on all this? Isn't this supposed to be a book about getting our joy back? I'm doing it because almost *nobody* responding to the survey admitted to being frustrated with themselves in response to this whole parenting-a-child-with-special-needs situation, remember? If hardly anybody is officially going on record as struggling—although I've talked with hundreds of women over the years who've verbally admitted that they are—I'm seeing the need for a little straight-on telling it like it is. Friend, if you're reading this and see yourself in this picture of brokenness, you aren't alone. You're not. None of us are. And because of that, we can take each other's hands and begin together to come out of hiding and into healing—a journey that begins when we forgive ourselves.

WE CAN RUN, BUT WE CAN'T REALLY HIDE

Your grief isn't invisible. And you aren't crazy. This survival business really is hard stuff, and you amaze me. As Mark Twain eloquently reflected, "Nothing that grieves us can be called little: by the eternal laws of proportion a child's loss of a doll and a king's loss of a crown are events of the same size."[6] So how we see ourselves in this role of parenting children with special needs and whether or not we learn to grieve the big and little things well comes down to one word: *grace.*

Grieving what we should have done sooner, might have done better, could have discovered earlier, or would have tried "if only . . ."—all of it needs to be wrapped into this one attribute of God.

Grace.

It's the part of Him that embodies our understanding that humanity is never good enough, that we will never be *enough* in and of ourselves to merit His love and sacrifice, and that what we do or don't do isn't the point. God knows we're dust (Psalm 103:14). Not that He thinks of us as dirt, something to trample upon and kick away, but that His expectation of us is realistic, based on our being created beings who haven't had a historically awesome track record. Scripture puts it another way: "We are all infected and impure with sin. When we display our righteous deeds, they are nothing but filthy rags" (Isaiah 64:6 NLT). God sees us, and He loves us entirely, in and in spite of our yuck. In and despite our mistakes, missed chances, and misunderstood moments.

He offers us forgiveness for every intentional sin, every accidental one, and even the ones we have no idea we've lived out. Nothing we have or haven't done in our lives—or for or to our special kids—either merits or disqualifies us from His love for us (Romans 8:28). The only aspect that hinges on us is this: will we receive it? Because that's what "forgiving ourselves" is all about. As psychology professor and author Dr. Everett L. Worthington Jr. states, "Self-forgiveness requires making a decision to value ourselves the way God values us."[7]

God sees us, and He loves us entirely, in and in spite of our yuck. In and despite our mistakes, missed chances, and misunderstood moments.

We don't have the power to acquit ourselves of what we've done or thought we've done wrong. We can't settle our sin issue with God on our own terms. The distance between us and our holy God is too vast to be surmounted by any effort we can muster. But that's why grace is so amazing. It's His grace that stretched a hand across a humanly un-crossable separation and pulled us to Himself: "But God demonstrates his own love for us in this: While we were still sinners, Christ died for us" (Romans 5:8).

Did you catch that verb tense? Paul says "demonstrates," not "demonstrated." He stated it a long time ago, but it's an offer for today. Or for the struggles of yesterday or of a few moments ago. For right now. For five minutes from now when you feel disappointed in yourself, give in to that anger flashpoint, or wish you could run away forever from the complexity of your special family. All God requires is that we accept His gift without mentally attaching strings that aren't there—that we acknowledge that, even if we aren't functioning anywhere near our "best" (whatever that may be this side of heaven!), we need God's grace. The moment we say "Yes, Lord. You're right. Even my best efforts are a mess, but you make beauty of all of it. Thank you for your grace," it comes pouring into our lives. And what a quality of life it ushers in! How it changes us, opens us wide to goodness instead of defeat.

It's in that moment when we accept and receive His grace that healthy grief makes way for joy in who we are, right here in the midst of our special families. And that's where the fun can really start.

PRACTICING SELF-FORGIVENESS

- Treasure truth. Create a collection of Scriptures in a journal or on note cards that remind you that you're forgiven by God. Over time add the dates of when you've declared your acceptance and thanks for each one.
- Invest in a good twelve-step resource. As parents of children with special needs, we may or may not be dealing with addictions we've used to cope with the stress. But we're all dealing with the codependency invited by our child's constant needs and dependence on us. Titles such as *The Twelve Steps—A Spiritual Journey: A Working Guide for Healing Damaged Emotions* by Friends in Recovery or *Codependents' Guide to the Twelve Steps* by Melodie Beattie bring to bear trusted recovery wisdom on the issues that keep our caregiver hearts all tied up in knots.
- Find and join a caregiver support group, online forum, or blog community. I write alongside thirty ministry leaders and authors—all of us parents of kids with special needs as well—at SpecialNeedsParenting.net. The site shares daily encouragement, Scripture, honesty, hope, and ideas to care for us parents as we care for our kids. On Facebook, I can recommend (in)Courage's community called (in)Able: moms of kids with special needs[8] as a place to share, find support, and pray with other moms around the world who get you. Whether you stop by those, find another online or in-real-life support space, or start your own, get connected. The support among members in these groups provides safe space to practice living in the freedom of forgiveness and grace with others seeking to do so too.

Three

RESTORING JOY IN HOW YOU SEE YOURSELF

"Forgiveness . . . cuts all the ties that prevent you from discovering who you were intended to be from the very beginning."
— Suzie Eller

I'm going to tell you something now, and you might want to sit down before I do: You still matter. And not just matter—*you are precious.*

Author and speaker Julie Barnhill reminds us that this is true, even amidst painful circumstances: "God watched over our construction from toes to fingertips to hair roots, and he has designed each of us to be exquisite, unequaled, and beyond compare. But it will always be our choice to live our lives as ourselves—not as someone we're not."[1]

This is probably the area of our biggest internal disconnect as parents of kids with special needs. As believers, we know at our core that we're unique, special. But our circumstances stomp all over us. The reality of "me" is so far underneath the pile of soiled laundry from our incontinent child that we can't even remember what it feels like to dream, or love ourselves, or to capture the vision of how precious we are as individuals to our Father's doting eyes. We get trapped in "There must be something wrong with me" instead of thriving in the recognition of what's *right* with (and within) us—of the beauty God wove into the *who* He chose for us to be. How, then, do we restore joy in that haggard self we see in the mirror?

DISCOVER WHO GOD MADE YOU TO BE

Whether we think of it often or not at all, there's a part of us deep down that longs to know why we're here—not only why we're alive but why we find ourselves *in this life right now.* In my book *Why Your Weirdness Is Wonderful*, I share, in detail, ways to discover answers to those existential questions by uncovering and developing our personal strengths—and (sometimes more importantly) discovering the hidden strengths in the aspects of ourselves we've often considered mistakes or weaknesses. This issue is worth a brief discussion here, since without a better understanding of the beauty God wove into each of us as individuals, joy can remain for us illusive, just out of reach.

So who are you? The psalmist says that you're "fearfully and wonderfully made" (Psalm 139:14). Do you recognize that reality every day, in yourself and in the interactions and situations you face? Do you have a sense of what makes you uniquely able to reflect the heart of God in the relationships in which you engage? Here are some questions to assist you in discovering and growing those strengths. (Will you permit me to be life-coach-y for a minute? Don't overthink your answers. Go with your gut responses. You might be surprised at what God reveals to you!) Grab paper and something to write with, and let's get started.

Abilities: What are you really good at? What do you do well with little effort? What comes naturally to you? What are you known for, whether others appreciate it or tease you about it?

Preferences: What do you love to do? What activities energize you? What sparks your curiosity, your attention, your loyalty, or your longing? With what people or organizations do you most enjoy interacting? During what part of the day are you most vital and creative? And in what environment do you work best? What do you like about that place—the lighting? The aroma? The quiet milling of people around you (or the total silence and lack of competing stimulation)?

Experiences: What are your most delightful memories? What feelings do they bring up? What was it about those events that made them so important or special? How have they changed you?

Now, what to do with all this introspection? This will be the fun part—the get your joy back part! Your mission, should you choose to accept it, is this: at least once a day, make it a point to lean in to those aspects of *you* that you've just (re)discovered. Decide to do one thing you love every day. Decide to regularly interact with one person or organization you enjoy. When considering opportunities to help in your child's classroom, at church, or elsewhere, opt for those interactions that will maximize your ability to do what's natural or easy for you because you're good at it.

Your mission, should you choose to accept it, is this: Decide to do one thing you love every day.

Is it selfish to intentionally plan for activities that optimize your strengths or make you happy? My friend, author, and fellow life coach Holley Gerth, addresses that question in this way: "Sometimes we feel guilty for wishing we knew more about ourselves. After all, we're not supposed to focus on ourselves, right? I often hear women say, 'That's selfish.' But it's not the question that matters—it's *what we do with the answer*."[2] It's all about what we do with our giftedness, which boils down to *who we love with it*. It's about accepting that the point of any strength God has given us is to better enable us to accomplish what Jesus identified as the point of it all: "You shall love the Lord your God with all your heart and with all your soul and with all your mind and with all your strength' . . . [and] 'You shall love your neighbor as yourself'" (Mark 12:30–31 ESV).

We love God and others best (and this includes our special kids) when we live intentionally within the core strengths of the unique and special *who* God designed each of us to be. John Eldredge emphasizes this truth in his book *Waking the Dead: The Glory of a Heart Fully Alive*. He encourages readers to get real, to choose to live bigger than we often allow ourselves to do—to live, as the title suggests, with a heart fully alive instead of one that's sleep-walking through God's adventures. He writes, "You cannot love another person from a false self. You cannot love another while you are still hiding. . . . You cannot love another unless you offer [him or her] your heart."[3] We can't offer something we don't have. If we're totally out of touch with the heart of who God designed us to be, no amount of serving or giving will make up for that. Allowing ourselves to consider, learn about, and grow the strengths God has given us cultivates the fully-alive heart—and the joy-filled life.

LET YOURSELF DREAM AGAIN

We never feel as though there's enough time to accomplish what needs to get done, do we? It would be so easy to ignore the concept that there might be more to our lives than our callings as parents of special kids. Even if we allow ourselves space to objectively consider our giftings, that may be as far as we let ourselves get before the "you're being selfish" lie begins to creep in.

It really is a lie, friend. Do you think God has nothing more for you beyond what lies smack dab in front of you this instant? No other person (besides your special child) to encourage? No idea to implement? No ministry to inspire, conceive, or birth? No dreams at all?

What dreams did you have as a child? As a student? After high school? Before marriage and family . . . and those monopolizing special needs? What desires have flitted through your mind in moments alone, or as you've listened to a favorite song, or in conversations with friends? We may not feel as though life gives us space to dream, but the dreams are nonetheless there, just below the surface. And joy awaits us right there with them, ready for us to grasp as we take the risk to dream again.

Perhaps you're responding, "Of course God has plans for me. I've got dreams. It's just not a good time to pursue them." That may be true. I've been there, many times. God sometimes does call on us to wait to pursue a dream that's in our hearts—like when our kids experience an uptick in their needs, when they're young, or when they go through a medical or mental health crisis. But that's just it: the waiting is for a season. At some point we must be willing to let ourselves dream again; to step out in faith to see God begin to flesh out that dream with reality; to try, fail, and try again, growing as we pursue a desire God Himself has placed in our hearts.

In her book *You're Made for a God-Sized Dream,* Holley Gerth encourages us not to let the "My family needs (all of) me" belief become an excuse when a dream is brewing and we sense it might be the time to act: "At some point we have to decide that the time for our dream is now. Because in today's world, normal never comes. There's always more to do, another 'when I . . .' to check off the list, another urgent demand to be met."[4]

It's true that normal never comes. Want to know how I know? Because you're reading a book I began to write the year my second daughter's mental health declined so sharply that she ended up in multiple psychiatric hospitals. The same year that, in a moment that nearly ripped out my mama heart, we made the painful choice to place her in a residential treatment facility. That wasn't a convenient or judicious time to write a book. It wasn't a normal season for our family (as if we've ever had one!). The very month our daughter transitioned back home after a year and a half at the facility I received the publishing contract for this book in the mail. This book—a dream I'd entertained for years, and one I wasn't at all sure I could handle given our family situation—began to become a reality. Right in the middle of not-normal and not convenient. Because dreams don't run the course of logic.

Dreams are God-sized, as Holley Gerth points out, not human-sized. They're inspired by the One who in a single week of out-loud brainstorming created our universe from nothing. By the same One who dreamed of redeeming it once humanity spit in His eye in the garden, who conceived the audacious plan of sacrificing His Son for its renewal. It was hardly convenient for God to give His Son for our atonement, or for us to have made a mess of things in the first place. After that no-doubt strenuous work of conceiving and actualizing a universe, the Creator could just as well have sat back and enjoyed the angels in heaven instead.

Fortunately for us, God remains in the business of dreaming. He wants to dream with you again. Will you let Him?

God remains in the business
of dreaming. He wants to
dream with you again.

SEEK OUT SUPPORTIVE "MIRRORS"

If stress is our silent killer, unrealistic expectations are its abettors. To get back our joy in the way we see ourselves, we have to better manage our inward expectations. As LJ, the mother of a nine-year-old child with Pervasive Developmental Disorder NOS explains, "I felt his recovery was completely up to me, that I needed to try to find just the right therapies, therapists, etc. . . . and I always felt I wasn't doing enough. Pretty much felt like I was losing my mind since there is such an overwhelming amount of information online and 'therapies' that everyone wants to [recommend]."

If you're like me, you may have read that and thought one part "been there, done that" and another part "Geez, lady, take it easy on yourself. You're getting a little intense!" But in a culture of instant information and guilt-tripping commercials that ask the dangling question, "You want the best for your child, right?" it's easy to lose perspective on what's reasonable for one person to do. Easy to feel inadequate for not trying everything available, easy to feel as though others are judging us for our every deficiency.

But when we find some clear mirrors in which to gaze, we can get realistic, get back our joy, and share it with other parents strapped by unrealistic self-expectations. I've gone through this process repeatedly throughout the years by enlisting people I trust—people who are willing to listen to what I'm doing or not doing—to objectively help me discern whether there are any holes in the current treatment/routine or, if not, to help me find ways to pull back into reality. One single mom with whom I talked mentioned that this approach was a life saver for her while raising a child with juvenile arthritis. She emphasized the value of trusted friends functioning as her objective sounding board. In her words, "People who didn't know anything about the disease were my biggest supporters. They didn't try to figure it out or tell me what to do. They let me talk through whatever [treatment] decision I had to make."[5]

As she talked, especially to people who didn't understand her daughter's disease, she could almost hear her own thinking process—what made sense to pursue and what didn't; what was or was not realistically possible.

What about those of us who don't have access to resources like that? How are we to maintain sanity and joy in our expectations of ourselves? Truth is, all of us have Someone to turn to. Jesus said so when He ascended to heaven after His death and resurrection: "I will ask the Father, and he will give you another Helper, to be with you forever, even the Spirit of truth" (John 14:16–17 ESV). This same Helper can be the sounding board we need, can give us wisdom about what's necessary, what's important, what's unimportant, and what's totally unnecessary as we care for our kids and organize our lives. We need only ask for wisdom, as Scripture promises: "If any of you lacks wisdom, you should ask God, who gives generously to all without finding fault, and it will be given to you" (James 1:5). It "will" be given, not it "might" be given. We can trust the Giver, listen for that counsel as we move through our day, our situations, our challenges.

ALLOW YOURSELF GRACE

Notice that I said "allow" not *give* yourself some grace? Because I'm not talking here about the dictionary definition of "favor . . . indulgence . . . temporary immunity or exemption."[6] No, not grace as in "Go ahead, self, eat that donut. You deserve it." (Not that I have anything against a good donut now and again.) What I am talking about is grace as the undeserved favor of God, a gift that we neither earn nor merit but that, when we open it, suffuses our lives with joy.

This is the grace to which the apostle Paul refers at the start of each of his biblical epistles: "Grace and peace to you from God our Father" (1 Corinthians 1:3). Grace from God to us. Grace from the One who loves us so dearly He was willing to sacrifice everything to redeem us. Grace that cuts through our experience into the muck of today and even through our crazy ways of viewing ourselves.

It's this grace that gave a mother permission to be vulnerable (John 19:26). That restored an outcast after her mistake (John 8:7). That touched—and in the process healed—society's "untouchables" (Luke 8:48). That calmed the storm, even when the distraught disciples suffered from a deplorable faith deficit (Luke 8:24–25).

It's this same grace that gives us permission to be vulnerable. That forgives us when we mess up. That respects and honors our grief, protects us and our families even when our faith is struggling, and touches us when we're so upset with ourselves *we* wouldn't go near us with a ten-foot pole. Grace that ushers in something we need in our minds and hearts more than just about anything else: peace. Dallas Theological Seminary grad and pastor J. Hampton Keathley expresses it this way: "Until we know and appropriate grace, we can't experience peace."[7]

So let's get to know it and choose to appropriate it. Let's get back our joy as we gaze into God's mirror and begin to understand what—let's make that *whom*—He sees when He looks at us. It's all about His grace. His unmerited favor. A gift that cost Him everything, a gift that's ours for the taking in the moments when we feel insecure, inadequate, overwhelmed, overextended, overlooked, or just plain *over it*. A gift that reconnects us with His heart for us, that reminds us in the midst of everything we're managing that we're so precious in His eyes, we're worth loving like crazy.

Four

WHEN SPECIAL NEEDS DON'T FEEL SPECIAL (FORGIVING YOUR CHILD)

I soak in the sunshine as I push my youngest on the park swing. My older daughter sits at the edge of the playground, mumbling, pulling out strand after strand of her hair. I've at least gotten her to sit quietly there, instead of the raging that was happening moments before. Another mom walks up and plops her child in the swing next to mine. She turns to me, and as much as I will her not to say it—as much as I wish I could take the words I know she's going to say and kick them into outer space—the words come anyway: "You must be really special. It takes someone amazing to raise a special needs child!"

No matter how many times I hear this—and I know you've heard it too—I never know what to say back. Of all the possible responses, the only one I can count on is guilt: "If only you knew some of the things I think about my child."

Thoughts like . . .

They don't make enough TUMS in the world to deal with your moods.

I'm embarrassed to be your parent when you act like that in public.

Why the heck won't you respond nicely when I try to help you?

I'm tired of doing [insert simple task] for you. I wish you could grow up.

I don't think I can go on doing this forever. . . sometimes I wish I didn't have to.

Those are pretty intense things to say . . . and to feel. And yet, as the parent of a special needs child, you've probably felt one or more of these in the past twenty-four hours. In fact, you may feel pretty badly about yourself and what you think of your child most days. In raising my younger, "typically developing" (whatever that means) kids, I know experientially that all parents feel this way at times. But when it comes to our special child, there's that added layer of guilt: the they-have-extra-challenges-so-I-must-be-a-jerk-to-think-like-that layer.

From our first moments with a child with special needs, we know both intense joy and intense pain. Within months of beginning to establish a relationship, we need to forgive our kids. Not because they've done something wrong but because we need to let go in order to thrive—to have joy again and to truly live, no matter what our child is facing or what that may mean for our families. It's true with all of our children, whether they cause grief as a "typical" toddler or thirty-four-year-old dependent in a wheelchair: We must let go of the resentment—that condition of wishing things were different—in order to do the real work of loving and raising our kids.

IT'S TIME TO GET HONEST

Where does all that resentment come from? For me it's multifaceted, but the source, beyond our grief over that disconnect between our expectations of life and its reality, is basically . . . us.

Seem over-simplified? Bear with me.

The real problem behind our resentment is that our hearts—the hearts of every human—are, as the Bible says, "the most deceitful of all things, and desperately wicked. Who really knows how bad it is?" (Jeremiah 17:9 NLT). Even us "saint-like" parents of special needs kids aren't exempt! To our credit, we work longer, harder hours than some other parents do. But our hearts—the core of our thoughts, emotions, and will—are no different from those of the worst people on earth we can imagine.

We know this, deep down, if we're being honest. My admissions at the start of this chapter reveal it: the impatience, the judgment, the self-pity, the fear, the anxiety, the anger.

You and I, in our grieving, hold on to those things just a little too long.

Because somehow being angry at our children for how much they need from us is strangely giving us energy—a thing we always need more of. We rely on that lack of forgiveness, however deeply we've stuffed it down inside, to help keep us going. It's easier to nurse resentment than to allow ourselves to feel pain, guilt, sadness, or fear. Reacting in this alternative way gives us a false sense of strength and competence when life is swirling out of control all around us. But really, where does it get us in terms of *relationship*? From where I sit, resentment is a recipe for building walls that do nothing in the long term but keep us isolated and leering at the world. Starting with the kids that make up so much of our experience of it.

Friend, we have to let this go. Even if it leaves us feeling vulnerable, disarmed. It's in setting down the false shield of resentment—in admitting our unreasonable expectations and the internal baggage we bring to the relationship—that we take the first steps in forgiving our kids, allowing ourselves to grieve in healthy ways, and living the life of joy we crave so intensely. This shift puts us in the best possible place to see our children, their behavior, and their needs in a gracious, realistic way. And beyond that, to truly *live* again in the face of what may be the hardest assignment we could ever have imagined as a parent.

Let's stop sugarcoating or qualifying how we feel or why we feel that way. Honesty about what frustrates and bothers us doesn't make us bad parents. It makes us moms and dads who care about being the best we can be for our children. Can you identify with these hurts that parents have shared with me about their special needs child(ren)?

They take time away from siblings or dominate the family.

As one mom put it, "The hardest thing for me as a parent is not allowing my son with special needs to take up all of my time and energy. Having four boys and being a military wife keeps me very busy. And I feel as though I have to devote more than 50 percent of my time and energy toward my son with special needs."

What does that really look like? Why is this a forgiveness issue with our special child, as opposed to an issue about which we'd do better to raise our eyes and shake our fists at heaven? A recent slice of my own life illustrates this:

I hit "answer" for the incoming call on the minivan's display. It was my oldest daughter's school, or, rather, her calling from the school. "Odd," I thought. "Why not call me from your own phone?"

"Mom, are you coming to get me?" I heard the anxiety in her voice, and with good reason since I was running late. Except that I had texted her before school let out that I'd be fifteen minutes late because I was shopping for something my preschooler needed for class.

"I texted you, honey. Did you get that?" I asked.

"No. I don't have my phone. I couldn't find it before school," she said, her voice calming.

I explained what happened, apologized, and hung up.

Fast-forward twenty minutes. We were home, and I asked where her phone was (she's a middle schooler, after all, and it isn't as though this would be the first time if it were lost).

"I looked everywhere this morning and couldn't find it. The charger was even missing from where I put it last night," she explained, but my mind already wondered whose little-sister hands caused this.

"My sister took my phone, I know it," she blurted. Deep down, I had a feeling she was right. This particular sister had taken so many things from the other girls without asking them; that's one of the things ADHD mixed with Reactive Attachment Disorder does in a family.

My heart sank, but my hope rallied: "We don't know that. Let's keep looking."

During the next two hours I comforted my oldest about the missing phone and the other times her sister had betrayed or taken things from her—like her entire bag of Halloween candy the week before. I was in intensive counseling mode with her, acknowledging how hard she'd tried and that it stinks that her sister is still acting out nine years after they both arrived in our family. I helped her see the other possibilities (like that she may actually have lost the phone) as we turned over the house in a futile search. And, yes, my younger two were home all the while, needing my help to get snacks, break up sibling squabbles, and focus and refocus on their homework. Multitasking at its most intense!

Two hours later: my oldest had her fear and anxiety in check, we'd gone through the house and called her carpool buddy to check their car, and the phone remained AWOL. In walked the suspect sister from after-school care (in which she'd been enrolled, ironically, so the family could have breaks from her being the one on which I focused so much energy).

My oldest said hello and asked her, "Have you seen my phone?"

This sister grabbed my oldest's hand, a look of sadness on her face, and lead her upstairs to reveal that she had hidden it in her room.

I won't go into the rage that knocked the wind out of me at that point, but suffice it to say it was time to do some work on forgiving this daughter. Again.

Some of you reading this know exactly what I'm talking about. Others aren't dealing with mental health and behavioral disabilities, so this isn't quite what you face. For you the issue may be complete physical exhaustion based on sleepless nights, days interrupted by calls to come help your child at school, thousands of hours of time at Children's Hospital, and texting your other kids at home when you'd rather be there with them in person to hear about their days or to play a board game.

The forgiveness issues are real with our special kids. Because sometimes special needs don't feel special at all; they feel more like a nightmare. It's okay to admit that; call the situation what it is; and then transfer all of that hurt, exhaustion, frustration, despair, and anxiety into the hands of God, who gives us the courage to let go.

Sometimes special needs don't feel
special at all; they feel more like a
nightmare. It's okay to admit that.

They require us to be constantly high-functioning or hypervigilant.

One of the hardest parts of parenting a special needs child and his or her sibling(s) is, as one mom put it, "Putting that smile on my face every day for [my kids] . . . Hiding my anger and frustration, hiding the 'pity pot' moments, and reminding myself to direct where it should go [so I can teach] them by example that everything will be okay, even though I haven't a clue either way."

That's one exhausting feature, tiring for its combination of battlefield-morale-builder and try-hard-mind-set (see the previous two chapters for more on the latter). It's a natural resentment builder, further compounded by the "preempting catastrophe" mode that is so common for parents of kids with mood, developmental, or behavioral disabilities. As one parent survey responder explained, "With a 'normal' child you can ignore small stuff they do, and it is a good strategy so you don't give attention to the negative behaviors and reinforce them. However, if I ignore my eleven-year-old daughter, she escalates and quickly becomes a serious threat or so unmanageable that it takes hours to calm her down. I have to be on her for little things with her behavior and nip everything in the bud. You just can't ignore anything."

That's stressful, people. As are the other issues parents shared that need our forgiveness:

For embarrassing us or their siblings in public—whether or not it's their choice.

For being mean when we give them so much of ourselves. Especially true for parents of children with special needs affecting mental and mood functioning.

For being so sick . . . for so long.

For dying. (Yes, this is part of the grieving process. It's okay to be mad at them for a moment, as irrational as your mind will tell you that is.)

All of these situations beg for the relief that begins with releasing the resentment they have built in us over time. This is a release that hinges on remembering who we ourselves are in our role as "children"—God's children.

HOPE FOR WHEN WE DON'T FEEL LIKE FORGIVING

As we've seen, it's our own need for and receipt of forgiveness that allows us to give to others in the same away. While He hung on the cross, Jesus in His dying breath pleaded, "Father, forgive them." There has never been a deeper grief caused by a child than that which our heavenly Father has endured with us as His broken, sinful people. It was you and me He was thinking of in that moment, as well as our kids and all the intensity that life with them brings. Thus, to begin the journey of forgiving our kids, we must once again, start by looking in the mirror.

After we've looked at ourselves and acknowledged our own need for forgiveness . . . what then?

Then we "just do it": we follow the biblical principle of doing, not just hearing, what's right. When we do the right thing, even from impure or still-hurt motives, we move toward the receipt of a changed (healed) heart. This is *really* good news for stressed-out parents of special needs kids. A simple step in God's direction takes us into living in His will and freedom.

Scripture encourages us, "Little children, let us not love in word or talk but in deed and in truth [purity of motive]. By this we shall know that we are of the truth and reassure our heart before him" (1 John 3:18–19 ESV). Will this kind of acted-out love be easy? Will we *feel* right at that instant as though we're free, as though we have truly forgiven? Probably not. But the Bible also encourages us in that "whenever our heart condemns us, God is greater than our heart, and he knows everything" (1 John 3:20 ESV). God knows we can only do so much. He simply asks us to take the first step and let Him help us the rest of the way.

The great news is this: as we continue doing what God asks us to do—the work of forgiving and letting go—the feelings will follow. When we simply step into the truth, we're already halfway there, and as we continue to allow God to work in us, our heart motives change and God is honored in the process (Philippians 1:18).

It boils down to this: active forgiveness is *doing* forgiveness. With our kids this means that we intend forgiveness before we get out of bed to face each day with them. We believe God's promise as we go about doing what He has asked us to do; we believe that He'll fill in the gaps and "help our unbelief" (Mark 9:24). When we walk in forgiveness moment by moment, regardless of how our kids' behavior, needs, or words make us feel, we're functioning as parents who honor God and respond to His love and forgiveness in our lives.

Active forgiveness is *doing* forgiveness. It means we intend forgiveness before we get out of bed to face each day with our children.

PRACTICING FORGIVING YOUR KIDS

- Reframe your experience of your child. Step back and look at it more objectively; include visualizing yourself from their perspective and trying to see things as they do/did in those hurtful moments. As author and speaker Suzie Eller describes in her book *The Unburdened Heart*, with those who can't change or reconcile in ways we would like, we can institute reframing forgiveness—what she calls *kaphar* forgiveness (so named after the original Greek word for "atonement"). Eller explains this kind of forgiveness in this way: "Sometimes the divide between you and someone who has created havoc in your life may seem impossible to overcome. . . . That's where *kaphar* forgiveness comes in to create a fresh start."[1] What could be harder to atone for than the wounds made by our kids who often don't understand why their neediness, behavior, or responses hurt us? By employing *kaphar* forgiveness with our child, we follow the model of what Christ did to satisfy the penalties of our own sin: we declare it finished. We wipe the ledger clean and, in doing so, allow for deeper relationship with our children and with the God who went before us in that sacrifice.

- Make some space for yourself both physically and emotionally. Plan this regularly, whether it be taking a nap, getting respite care, breathing in a favorite scent, or meeting a friend for coffee. If that isn't possible, plan for less frequent longer periods away when you can. Sometimes it has taken me three hours to begin to relax when I go away. On other occasions it's been ten minutes. Make space as often as possible—in as many little ways as possible—to refresh and recharge so you can give yourself a fighting chance at joy.
- Make the personal connection. Every time you're frustrated with your child, consider a time you've been that frustrating kid to God. Confess your displeasing moment to God. Let Him make the memory of what once was negative and childishly sinful into a new moment of redemption. Allow yourself to breathe in His grace and forgiveness.

Five

REDISCOVERING JOY WITH YOUR SPECIAL CHILD

We're expert advocates for our kids at school, at church, and in the community. But back at home we all can get pretty frustrated with them and the intense lives their needs create. It has taken a lot of honesty for me to admit that, given the choice, I'd rather clean my house than engage my hardest-to-raise child in any given moment.

Something had to change. And that something was the need to stop *reacting* and start *responding* to the challenges once again. As we choose to forgive, we're freed and enabled to do just that. Forgiving moves us from reacting to and controlling our children out of sheer exhaustion to being their ultimate first responder. Just as nurses, doctors, and emergency medical technicians come into a situation trained and prepared to support those in need, we can be our child's first responder as we're on the scene, helping them meet their own needs and manage their feelings. We can come alongside them as partners and mentors in *their* journey— not as people who solve their problems for them. We can choose to take care of ourselves in the midst of helping our child instead of jumping into "self-defeating, learned survival behaviors"[1] that we've developed to cope with our children's needs.

Joy comes when we deliberately decide to be in charge of our own emotions once again, and as we let go of our expectations that our kids will respond like we want them to. It happens when we ban the word *should* from our vocabularies and when we empathize with our kids instead of feeling personally attacked by their needs or behaviors. That's a hard thing for a day-in-and-day-out caregiver to do! It's much easier to opt for the familiar sense of being out of control. But if we're honest, it's the only way we'll feel safe enough to engage powerfully in our lives as special needs parents and beyond. Let's dig in and see how this works in our pursuit of joy with our special kids.

Joy comes when we deliberately
decide to be in charge of our own
emotions once again, and as we let
go of our expectations that our kids
will respond like we want them to.

USE LIFE-GIVING, INSTEAD OF LIMITING, WORDS

I'm not talking about the kinds of words you no doubt carefully say or don't say when you talk about your child's conditions in public (or even just with friends and family). What I'm talking about here is how you *think* about your child. What words do you use in your self-talk to describe her? Or your situation? Or his needs? Do any of these ring a bell?

Dependent	Irritable
Demanding	Tiring
Needy	Whiny
Fragile	Extreme
Aggressive	Explosive
Stuck	Stubborn

When it comes to our kids, it's easy to find ourselves using terms like these. I know I have (a lot), especially in those end-of-the-day debriefings with my husband. Parenting author Mary Sheedy Kurcinka, having raised her own intense son and worked with many other parents, came up with a new term for intense kids—kids she says were privately described by their parents as "difficult, strong-willed, stubborn, mother killer, or Dennis the Menace."[2] Kurcinka called them *spirited children*. And with that single shift—that brilliant reframe in perspective—she made it possible for exhausted parents to like their kids again.

Kurcinka shares, "Spirited children possess traits 'in the raw' that are truly valued in adults but challenging to live with in a young child."[3] Traits like tenacity (stubbornness), curiosity (getting into trouble), questioning the status quo (argumentative), sensitivity (whining), connectedness (clinginess), and communication (chatterbox). This perspective shift can change our lives, moving us from frustration in trying to make our kids different from who they are, to experiences in partnership, in which we're functioning more as detectives than police officers—on the alert for ways to build on what's good in our kids and to help them do the same.

Joy grows as we shift focus and readjust our role in engaging with these challenging aspects of who our kids are. It multiplies when we choose, as Kurcinka advises in her workshops, "to examine the negative labels we use to describe our kids and change them." Why? Because as we actively let go of resentment through thinking and speaking more life-giving words about our kids, we discover the truth: "In every single one of those behaviors [attitudes, challenges] is a potential strength."[4]

I see Kurcinka's point often, not only in my own family but also as I coach individuals and families. It's clear that the words we use speak either life or death into those around us. They either limit or invite other people's strengths (or even our own, based on how we see ourselves).

The words we use speak either life
or death into those around us.
They either limit or invite other
people's strengths.

If we look at a challenging behavior or need in our child and label it with descriptors like "whiny," "difficult," "rebellious," "demanding,"

"irrational," or "impossible," we're only going to see it in that light. As someone once said, "To a hammer, everything looks like a nail," right? If we instead choose to look at those tendencies as "seeking to connect," "determined," "sensitive," or "a chance for us to grow," we invite joy back into the relationship. We let our kids off the hook and give them space to develop those attributes as strengths rather than keeping them tied to the debilitating versions.

HELP THEM—AND THEIR SIBLINGS—PROCESS THE STRUGGLES AND LOSSES

We're not the only ones grieving in our families. Our kids with special needs grieve as they discover over time that they function differently from their peers. Their siblings grieve the limitations their sister or brother experiences and the loss of attention from us. All of them struggle with frustration, isolation, and not being able to do the things or go to the places they want some (or most) of the time. Now, just in case the thought of having to engage not just your own grief makes you want to run far, far away and not come back, may I say it again?

You are not alone.

The thought of adding another responsibility to the list of care we give as parents can feel like an elephant sitting on our heads. But here's the thing: *not* processing grief—theirs or ours—is asking the elephant to move in and live on our heads forever. Grief authors John W. James and Russell Friedman, in their bestselling guide, *The Grief Recovery Handbook*, explain, "While grief is normal and natural, and clearly the most powerful of all emotions, it is also the most neglected and misunderstood experience, often by both the grievers and those around them."[5] These authors have seen firsthand in their thirty years of work with people that what hurts us most as people is not grieving itself, but ignoring it. They cite the oft-shared sentiment, "Time heals all wounds," and turn it on its head, saying, "Time itself does not heal; it is what you do within time that will help you complete the pain caused by loss."[6] *Complete the pain.* To be able to complete anything is a delicious concept as a caregiving parent! To be able to complete and move past something as exhausting as pain? All I can say is, "Yes, please!"

As we support our children with special needs and their siblings in grieving their losses, we find more opportunities for delight and more energy to face our own needs. This journey to joy begins as we give our kids permission to think—and talk with us—about what's bothering them, which means we can be the ones who bring up the topic. That will look different for each child, but it's our job to open the door if they don't. Open-ended statements or questions like "I wonder how you feel when your brother acts like that at school," or "Do you ever wish you could run like that—unassisted?" tell our kids we notice their struggles. That no matter what it is they're struggling with, it's important and valid. Recognition like that invites joy not just in our kids but in our relationships with them.

Beyond that, we can help them recognize their grief feelings and behaviors—manifestations like changes in diet, friendships, or level of aggression. Set limits with things that damage people or property, but beyond that give them words for what they feel so they can learn to choose new options instead of challenging behaviors. When my girls rage, bicker, sneak, steal, or damage something, it's my cue to start observing their behavior out loud with statements like "Wow, that was a big reaction to something not so big. I wonder what's behind that? I think I'd be sad (or mad, or frustrated, or hurt . . .) about (whatever you suspect to be the issue)." As we acknowledge the behaviors and help our kids reframe what's going on in their thoughts and feelings, we open the door a little wider to mutual joy.

In addition, we can teach our kids to recognize grief signs in their bodies. As an adult we may identify tense shoulders as symptoms of emotion, but kids will simply feel yucky. Share where anxiety lives: in the head (thoughts, headaches), stomach (changed appetite, nausea, pain), heart (increased heart rate/breathing), and shoulders (tension). Live your own feelings "out loud" as you go through your day so they can see this modeled. Verbalize your moment-by-moment reactions and responses, like "That guy just cut in front of me on the freeway—that scared me. My heart's really racing!" The more we model, the more they adopt those healthier ways of coping, and the more the whole family can get its joy back.

ACCEPT MORE OF THOSE THINGS THAT BUG YOU

Acceptance is another way we get back our joy with our kids—and probably the most powerful for our own peace of mind. Terri Mauro, author of *50 Ways to Support Your Child's Special Education* and editor of the website "Mothers with Attitude," stumbled upon a brassy and poignant idea on a T-shirt. It changed her view of her adopted child who is hindered by difficult behaviors associated with fetal alcohol syndrome. The nugget of T-shirt wisdom she found? "The more of my behavior you accept, the less you will have to forgive."

Mauro shares her reaction to the idea in this way:

> That [quote] speaks of choosing your battles. Targeting only those behaviors that are truly unacceptable, and ignoring the ones that are merely annoying. Understanding that, as much as you want certain behaviors to change, your child is not able to do that at this time, or maybe ever. Harnessing your energy, and loving your kid warts and all.[7]

When, as Mauro encourages, we let go of the need to exact a punishment and focus instead on controlling the behavior or the intensity of our child's needs, we can reel in a little more joy. To accept doesn't mean to ignore, as Mauro emphasizes. When we ignore the unacceptable, it can incite more craziness and build bad habits. But when we demonstrate our forgiveness for our kids through accepting some of the behaviors that rub us the wrong way but aren't empirically hurtful—simply as a way of honoring who they are, differences and all—life somehow gets less crazy. It's a win-win situation and a way to grow joy in our families.

What does that look like? In practice it looks like curiosity. When it comes to the things that bug us most about our child's behaviors or quirks (or about our own, our spouse's, or anyone else's for that matter), joy happens when we stop trying to avoid or fix those quirks, and instead ask God for eyes to see what He intended when He wired them that way. Because Scripture states that we're fearfully and wonderfully made. That's a promise as well as an admission. Those things we hate about our kids or ourselves? They're intrinsic within these complex and wonderful personalities, and joy comes as we start to let ourselves see the wonder God has wired into those very traits.

Joy happens when we stop trying
to avoid or fix our child's quirks,
and instead ask God for eyes to see
what He intended when He wired
them that way.

PLAY EVEN IF YOU DON'T WANT TO (YET)

It was Halloween week, and even without the sugar rush I was dreading, my kids were bouncing off the walls. All week my second-oldest daughter struggled with her homework, responsibilities, chores, and simple courtesy toward her sisters. There had even been an instance where she'd disappeared from the house for three hours when she was supposed to be confined in her room because she'd made a bad choice.

In other words, the fact that on that Friday night she was banned from the neighborhood fall festival wasn't news to the family. Nor was it unexpected, sad to say. As is our custom, my husband and I discussed who would take the kids who'd earned a trip to the festival, and who would stay home with my limit-testing girl. Mid-negotiations with my husband I stopped, told him to go have fun with the other kids, and waved them off for an evening of tricks and treats.

My daughter started up the stairs to her room, but I shocked us both by inviting, "Want to play a game?" Eyes widened, and she tentatively came back downstairs. We picked one of her favorites, unpacked it all over the kitchen table, and started a game that would end up lasting the full two hours before the rest of the family came home.

Why the heck did I do that with my kiddo with a penchant for sneaking out and pushing every limit? Because I needed to play!

And so do you.

We get so wrapped up in the intensity of caring for a challenging or fragile child that we just don't play much, especially (and detrimentally) with the child who's hardest on us. While we don't want to make a rule of playing when consequences are in order, making the exception can be just the thing the whole family needs to short-circuit the stress and jumpstart joy once again.

This was true that night with my daughter. As I tucked her into bed later on, she, of her own volition—a huge feat for a child with Reactive Attachment Disorder—apologized for each chore she'd skirted that week, as well as for the ways she'd been disrespectful or deceptive with me that day. She asked what she could do to make it up to me (and, even better, followed through the next day with those things we'd decided!).

Does it happen like that every time? Ha! I wish. But, seriously, when we've gone through the forgiving process, done some healthy grieving over our experiences with and expectations of our children with special needs, if that joy is still elusive may I recommend taking a play break? It may just give you that needed nudge toward restoring the positive feelings in relationship with your special child.

FOR BETTER OR FOR WORSE
(FORGIVING YOUR SPOUSE)

I read once that marriage is like being part of a mobile. You get the dress, write the vows, and promise the world at the wedding; then you wake up in the honeymoon suite to "Sweetie, let's watch Nascar," when the obvious choice would be the beach. Two people have been connected on the first rung of the mobile, and it swings wildly to find its center—to balance diverse needs and wants, to help find a middle ground on issues from date nights to bills to who's cleaning the bathroom this week. It takes a while to get the "swing" of things as a couple, but once you figure out how you balance each other out, the mobile settles into a gentle dance-like rhythm, and life is joyful and calm again.

When baby makes three, the mobile goes nuts. Sleepless nights, feeding challenges, spit-up, and diaper changes throw the marriage mobile totally out of whack for a while. Those issues work themselves out, and the mobile stabilizes into the new normal for your family. To one degree or another, this happens all over again with teething, toddlerhood, potty training . . . and the list goes on. But the point is that you expect it (even if you don't expect the "how" that sets the family to swinging again), and you know that with whatever passing phase, this too shall end. Maybe you've even gone through this particular dance before with an older sibling, so you *really* know it will end and can even help your friends gain perspective as they too swing around.

At some point the mobile settles down, days are quieter, everyone knows his or her spot in the family, and a measure of independence returns.

But what if the situation never stabilizes?

What if it stays cockeyed—the wire connecting you with your spouse sagging under the weight of your child with heavier needs and issues than you could ever have expected to manage? If the mobile never stabilizes, or if some new facet of your child's needs throws it into fresh chaos every few months, how do you go on functioning in perma-swing mode? How do you re-create your middle—your balance—as a couple? Because the longer you sway, the more seasick you get, and the more you just want to pack your bags, stop this crazy ride, and yell, "Let me off, already!"

You'll try to create a livable rhythm—find a center in the swaying—by focusing everything you have on that third, now not-so-new figure throwing the mobile out of whack. You try to ground it through nutrition, stabilize it with therapies, scoot it closer to your side of the mobile because . . . who knows? Maybe if your child is in *your* space all the time, the situation will mimic how it was when there were just you and your spouse. The strategy seems sound, and you feel hopeful it will work—this family mobile with two people (one adult and one demanding child) on your end and one person (the one you're supposed to be "with" in your marriage) alone and bewildered on the other.

After a while, with the swaying and constant focus on baby-now-child (or maybe teen or even adult), you look across and see a blur that you're pretty sure is your spouse. He or she seems different somehow . . . distant. But is it even possible to trust what you see with all that whipping around? You wonder, "What's that expression on his face? Is he judging me for how I'm doing with this kid here on my end? How dare he?! He should come over here on this side and see how it feels!"

From the other end, your spouse sees you too. Or at least someone who looks a little bit like you, albeit a bit more tired, distracted, and lost. And which part of that two-person end is you and which is the child? It's so hard to tell from way over there. So your spouse tries to reach across. You snap, "Why would you do that? Can't you see I've just about got things settled here?" Your spouse shrinks back, but later makes another tentative foray, inching closer this time—trying something new—and the mobile swings a little. You freak out (people working hard, well beyond what they actually have to give, tend to do that), and your spouse retreats back to the other side.

What else can your spouse do? Every time he or she tries something, it scares you so much you just want to make everything stop. Even your spouse. And eventually, that's exactly what can end up happening.

THE CHOICES WE ALL NEED TO MAKE

Your family's mobile is going to be lurching forever. It just is. So your choices as I see it are these: (1) work on the marriage, (2) ignore it and watch it fall apart, or (3) end it. To work on it will require effort, intention, a giant helping of grace, and faith that is truly "the substance of things hoped for [like unity and feeling supported], the evidence of things not seen" (Hebrews 11:1 NKJV). It will exhaust you some days, especially those days when your child already did. It may lead you to yell at God, who has the power to lighten your load, but instead allows you to have to work as hard at marriage as everyone else. Whatever it may require of you, choosing to work on your marriage will pay back a thousand-fold, in often unexpected ways. In our family, it's been on the days when my spouse surprises me by doing the soiled laundry, texting me when he knows I'm on the way to that dreaded meeting at the school, or bragging about me to the other couple with whom he set up a surprise double date so I could get out of the house and be his woman again for a few hours.

FOUR COMMON CHALLENGES IN MARRIAGES WITH A SPECIAL NEEDS CHILD

Whatever your unique situation or your child's challenges, you face the same marriage choice your friend with the calm, "normal" family mobile does. You and I might have to make that choice daily or even hourly because of the reality of being married to not only our spouse, but a fellow caregiver. This chapter takes a closer look at four common themes I've experienced in my own marriage, as have many of the survey responders for this project.

Whatever your unique situation or
your child's challenges, you face the
same marriage choice your friend
with the calm, "normal" family does.

Your spouse doesn't do their share with your special child.

Pick up any family magazine or marriage book, and you'll find tips for healthy marriages that include deciding fair distribution of household chores, figuring out the roles of wife and husband, communicating well, resolving conflict, making decisions together, and giving each other space when we're tired or work is stressing us out. All these are important for a healthy marital partnership. But when the work of parenting remains as intense for us as it is during only the first few years for a typical family, we want to rewrite the entire marriage book from scratch, from the point of view of "all bets are off, and it's everyone for him- or herself."

It's with that mind-set that we start to keep score—a problem for any marriage or partnership, and one that can escalate resentment through the roof in families like ours.

Here are a few ways you may be keeping score and adding up the infractions:

- Your spouse may attend some IEP meetings, doctor appointments, or therapist appointments, but the brunt of the preparation and attendance falls to you.
- Your spouse texts to ask whether you can pick up that extra item at the store, . . . with the kids that required that three-hour IEP meeting in tow. When you attempt to pick up a few other things you need, realizing only when your spouse asks that you forgot the item he had requested, you want to scream at him for making any requests at all.

- Your spouse does her best to spend time at home with the child, but her best is an hour, and after that she is tired—the child is hard work and she is already exhausted from her job, after all—so she hopes you'll understand when she goes to read or take a nap upstairs for a few hours. You don't understand. Not even a little.

- Your spouse wonders why you don't want to have sex later on when the kids are in bed, and all you can think in response is, "Listen, Nap-taker, don't even get me started!"

- Your spouse offers to help during those tense—and hopefully brief—intervals when you're sick, with things like filling prescriptions and doing the laundry and dishes. But you feel as though you have to be on the brink of death for the offer to materialize.

- And don't even get you started on whether your spouse actually picks up the prescriptions or finishes the dishes. Because that's a whole different rant.

If you could summarize this as a single thought, it would sound something like this: if you're going to be the primary caregiver, your spouse should be jumping in, offering help, and carrying at least 50 percent of the workload. Which is rarely how it happens.

Resentment, anyone?

Your spouse doesn't follow your child's care plan the way you want.

My husband often doesn't know the up-to-the-minute bipolar or ADHD management strategies for our girls (he's been busy working his hind end off to pay for us to have a house in which to behavior manage). But he wants to help and be involved, so he'll recommend strategies and behavior modification ideas. Trouble is, he (a) doesn't know the recently recommended strategies, and (b) I don't have the energy to sit and have a how-brains-with-bipolar-respond-to-traditional-parenting summit as my daughter's decompensating in the other room. So I do what any person in a war zone does: I deal quickly and effectively with the bomb and let the relationship with my husband wait its turn.

He notices that I didn't do what he recommended, and that I'm still struggling with the same things months later (because, apparently, these issues aren't something our kids outgrow?), so when I'm out one night with friends he uses his technique instead of the one the psychiatrist recommended. It's a good one . . . for a typically functioning child. A time-out with a chore in response to our daughter screaming at him. Hours later I return to find her disheveled, her room in chaos, and the problem about which she was trying to get my husband's help—really loudly and in a way only someone who understands how her mind works would catch—is still unresolved. She's crying. He's stressed and frustrated. I'm scared we've lost ground with her behavior and mood management. And I want to throw a rock at the guy on the other end of my rung of the mobile.

You feel your spouse is critical of how you manage your special child.

This one's especially prevalent in families with children who have "invisible disabilities"—behavior, mood, developmental, or mental health challenges that can look to an outsider like the result of negligent parenting. Since the spouse is over there on the far side of the mobile, they can feel a bit like an onlooker and, perhaps unintentionally, start to convey an outsider's view.

This happens in my family regularly. I'll have the day from hell with my two older girls—the one with RAD and ADHD soiling, lying, and stealing, and the other with bipolar and ADHD raging, accusing, and crying inconsolably. I'll use positive parenting techniques, coach my one child through cleaning up her messes and paying back the sister from whom she stole the item. I'll maintain healthy detachment from my moody child, helping her use her coping skills and take some personal space. I'll consequence bad behavior with chores the kids help brainstorm, and I'll even give myself a time-out when I'm about to lose it after all that high-level parenting. In other words, it was a mom day worthy of a Nobel Peace Prize.

But he doesn't know that. He may walk into the kitchen during the (witching) dinner hour, while I'm ignoring a meltdown so I can take dinner off the stove, and say something like, "Honey, are you seeing this? Didn't we say we were going to handle meltdowns by [whatever we'd agreed on]?" Which sounds to me an awful lot like, "Honey, you're a failure. What the heck have you been doing all day?"

That one moment breaks me more than hours of therapeutic, exhausting parenting with my girls, and I'm likely to just about lose it. Those instances make me want to grab my kitchen scissors and cut the mobile that's our whacky family to shreds. Because aren't we supposed to be partners in crime or something? Isn't he supposed to trust me with our kids and give me the benefit of the doubt? Maybe even rush to my rescue like Superman who, in one fell swoop, makes the whole wretched mess all better?

Your spouse seems oblivious to your struggles.

Perhaps you've heard of compassion fatigue? It's a condition in caregivers that Dr. Charles Figley, director of the Figley Institute (formerly Florida State University Institute of Traumatology), describes thus:

> The helper, in contrast to the person(s) being helped, is traumatized or suffers through the helper's own efforts to empathize and be compassionate. Often, this leads to poor self care and extreme self sacrifice in the process of helping. Together, this leads to compassion fatigue and symptoms similar to post-traumatic stress disorder (PTSD).[1]

If we have compassion fatigue (and we often do without realizing it), our spouses have secondary compassion fatigue. They have their own fatigue because of our children (even if we don't think they're engaged enough with them and the process), and they endure the backlash from ours. They're not only weary in co-parenting children who need more than they could ever have dreamed, they're weary of their spouses being in a world of hurt because of it. We're hurting in the midst of all the helping, and they're affected by our struggles.

If this seems implausible, consider another example. Perhaps you have a friend who's struggled for a long time with a certain issue. That struggle has lasted for a year, two years, or five years, and after a while you've prayed enough, listened enough, offered enough help (which your friend can't/doesn't take since it isn't exactly what's needed), and walked along-side enough. You're ready to move on, but your friend can't. In friend-ships, that scenario can necessitate a time apart—a little distance so you can recover and get your game back on to be a friend and supporter and engage once again.

Your spouse doesn't get to do that. But he or she does end up making space anyway—tuning out, working late, taking extra naps—because if being there for a needy child is exhausting, being there for the one who is supposed to be a life partner but who's wrapped in knots around your child's needs is twice as painful.

Maybe you've noticed other people doing that "distance" thing. A friend doesn't invite you and your child to her daughter's birthday party. People at church stop asking how you are. Teachers get a little less excited about your ideas to help your child in class. The church class helper is tired of managing this too-old-to-have-a-meltdown kid. In those moments you can almost understand. But with your spouse? No way. Your hus-band or wife doesn't get to react that way. Ever.

All of these issues leave us feeling alone in our own homes—misun-derstood, invisible, wounded, grieving. The mountain of resentment they build, when left undealt with, can eventually morph into the ava-lanche that crushes our joy or even breaks up our families.

THE GOAL: SETTING YOU BOTH FREE TO JUST . . . BE

When it comes to getting the mountain of resentment off your back, it's in this relationship above all others (except for the one with God) that it's crucial for you to do so. Because even if you have big resentments about your child or doctors or your extended family, it's your spouse you're waking up to every day. It's this person from whom you *can* expect big things, since your kids may not be capable of them and the rest of the world hasn't walked down the aisle and committed its lifetime to you as your spouse has. So how does that work? In the fifteen years my husband and I have been doing this marriage thing—during ten of which we've been raising kids with special needs—here are a few resentment-busting principles we've stumbled upon.

The Freeing Truth That Opens Doors to Healthy Marriage

When we met our spouses and then got engaged, we entertained fairy-tale notions of tackling the world together as a starry-eyed team. But round about the time we had our first fights during the wedding-planning phase, we started to get the hint: nobody's perfect. They're not perfect, and neither are we. As the former president of Mothers of Preschoolers International (MOPS), Elisa Morgan, acknowledges in her book *The Beauty of Broken*, "I'm broken. Everybody is. So no matter what we do, we all end up making broken families. In one way or another."[2] We all end up making broken marriages.

Forgiveness begins when we admit that we're also a mess. That we're all, as author Mary DeMuth puts it, "[walking] this earth with megachips on our shoulders, believing ourselves to be victims of everyone else's self-ishness. But the biblical truth is we all sin."[3] We've ignored what our spouses need. We've felt entitled to treatment we don't want to reciprocate. We expect our marriage partners to have bad days and still be the prince or princess from those fairytales. (Really, we expect them never to have bad days or, if they do, to automatically understand that ours was worse.)

Yes, we're exhausted; yes, we're overextended. Yes, it's okay to admit that we may have it harder than most—that our marriages might have it harder than most. But the truth is this: we made promises at that altar, and no matter how hard things are for us as parents, it's not okay to shirk those vows. This is what it means to live what we said: "to have and to hold from this day forward, for better for worse, for richer for poorer, in sickness and in health, to love, cherish, and to obey, till death us do part."[4] As our doe-eyed younger selves, neither my husband nor I under-stood what that meant, but after all these years together, we're messing up today just as badly as we did in those early stages. When we swallow our (understandable, yet utterly sinful) pride in this realization, forgive-ness can begin to flow.

The Hard Truth That Empowers You to Love Your Spouse

We live in an era where personal rights rule. Media, politicians, and even friends tell us that we deserve to have that dream house, dream spouse, dream body, and dream job. For those of us in the United States, our very country was founded on the premise that each of us "[is] endowed by [our] Creator with certain unalienable Rights, that among these are Life, Liberty and the pursuit of Happiness."[5] How happy are we, with all these rights we fight so hard to achieve and maintain? We're not too happy, friend. Some studies argue that the U.S. has the highest divorce rate in the world[6] and the second highest rate of depression.[7] Probably because, as author Cindi McMenamin notes in *When a Woman Overcomes Life's Hurts*, "When we believe we have a right to be happy, we're believing a lie that results in disappointment and disillusionment. Sometimes it even results in bitterness. But mostly it keeps us from a proper understanding of what it means to live as a follower of Christ."[8]

What *does* life look like for a follower of Christ? Quite honestly, it's the polar opposite of what our culture touts. The Bible teaches that we were born slaves to sin (Romans 6:17). When we came to faith we switched masters, and now we, "who were once slaves of sin . . . having been set free from sin, have become slaves of righteousness" (Romans 6:17–18 ESV).

The word *slave* has no positive connotations in our culture, but in the context of the times in which the Bible was written its meaning was simply this: one who is indebted. (Now *debt*, that's something we understand in this country!) We used to be indebted to the law God gave to govern human conduct and choices—the Ten Commandments—along with all those extra stipulations heaped on top of them by religious authorities. But once we admitted how utterly bankrupt that left us and chose to receive Christ's gift of *salvation* ("help" in the original Greek),[9] our debt changed hands. We now belong to God. Which is great news for all of us who feel stranded in our homes or marriages: since we're His, our livelihoods rest squarely in His hands. Or, as McMenamin later writes,

> If you live from this day forward with the knowledge and affirmation that you are His, you belong to Him, and you owe your life to Him, suddenly your needs, wants, and expectations are no longer your concern: they are His obligation. . . . Your life is no longer about your rights, your disappointments, your hurts. It's about His redemptive work in you.[10]

However we slice it, we are not our own. We owe our lives, souls, eternal destinies, care, and keeping—everything—to God. And that's good news when we're struggling with "It's not fair!" issues in our lives or marriages.

> We owe our lives, souls, eternal destinies, care, and keeping— everything—to God. And that's good news when we're struggling with "It's not fair!" issues in our lives or marriages.

What Your Spouse May Never Say (But Needs You to Know)

Our spouses may not show it. They may not talk about it (in my house that would be because I'm the one talking about it most of the time). They may not ask for our help, but they're struggling and tired too. I know this because my husband has many times looked across the couch at me during one of our daughter's intense moments and mouthed the silent words, "How in the world do we handle *this*?" I know because a friend Brian shared with me that he's grieving but won't tell his wife because she's working so hard with their autistic boys. I know because Greg Lucas, a police officer, author, and father of a grown son with autism, wrote this during a particularly hard night his son had:

> That night was long and dark and numb, I will forget it not.
> It emptied me of everything—of word, and strength, and
>   thought.[11]

I could write a whole book just about the experiences of fathers—the often secondary caregivers. Suffice to say they're scared, too—for themselves, their marriages, their children's prognoses. And they're angry that this is happening to their families. They're stressed as they work hard to provide financially for their families and shoulder the often extraordinary medical and therapeutic burdens. They feel irrelevant while we, the primary caregivers, have more of the daily experience, knowledge, and specialist information about our kids. They feel guilty. If the child is biologically theirs, they (like us) wonder: "What if it was me who 'did' this to my child?"

In other words, they're grieving, stressed, and scared. Just as we are. But they may not verbalize it . . . unless we honor their grief and give them space to say it. (We'll get into some ways to build that back into the relationship in the next chapter.) When we let our gazes linger a moment on our spouses, even in the most frustrating circumstances when we're feeling like strangers living together under one roof, compassion and empathy grow, opening the door to life-giving forgiveness in the relationship.

PRACTICING FORGIVING YOUR SPOUSE

- Observe your spouse. Look at your spouse when he or she doesn't know you're looking—maybe while he's sleeping next to you, maybe from across the room when she's trying to get your non-verbal child to convey his needs (and failing, as you sometimes still do). Make yourself keep looking—count to ten if you have to. What do you notice about your spouse? Does he or she look happy? Contented? Tired? Tense? The more descriptors you can think of as you observe, the better. Now pray according to what you've noticed. You can't pray observantly and *not* have compassion, so as it grows in your heart, seal it with the choice in that moment to forgive whatever negative event has happened today, yesterday, or this week.
- Go back to the drawing board. Begin a forgiveness journal about your spouse. Write or draw about your feelings connected (directly or indirectly) with things your spouse says or does. Next to each entry write about a time *you* did something similar, or record a Scripture reference that reveals God's forgiveness of your spouse.

When you struggle with feeling misunderstood, undervalued, judged, or alone, and the resentment starts to well up, pull out that journal and remind yourself of the truth—of what you've done, and of what God promises—and decide afresh to let go.

Seven

REKINDLING JOY WITH YOUR SPOUSE

"There is no reason why couples need to settle for a 'second-rate' marriage because they have a child with a disability."
—Dr. Laura E. Marshak, *Married with Special-Needs Children*

I hit the Send button to text my husband: "Another 30 min conversation with the school nurse. More 'have you tried . . . ?' I would really be OK never discussing our daughter's GI issues again. Ever." He texts me while just outside his meeting at work: "Want me to call you?"

"No, that's OK. I have to write, anyway," I text back.

"I'm calling," he replies; a hint of a smile forms on my lips.

He calls, and I don't want to talk, but he keeps dragging it out of me. He knows. Finally it comes tumbling out, and I tell him all the gory details of yet another long conversation, in which the well-meaning professional on the other end of the phone suggested that maybe, instead of the easy, doctor-recommended over-the-counter treatment I gave my daughter last week, I should make an appointment with the specialist next time her constipation occurs and then take her in for an abdominal x-ray.

To which my husband chimes in, "Or, you could drop a bowling ball on your foot. Neither of which you'd ever want to do . . ."

We both laugh. Hard. We've done this for too long . . . the gallows humor reveals it. But honestly, this is why I love him. And it's why I need to cultivate our relationship no matter how frustrated I get with everyone else in the world that's a part of the treatment for our older girls.

At one point I almost threw away this life with him. Years ago, after our third daughter was born, and a few years into foster parenting our older girls, the marriage was somewhere between complacent and downright hostile. We were both exhausted; our home had been turned upside down with the therapies, appointments, and parenting techniques our older daughters required. We were isolated from our friends and were both handling that badly. He immersed himself in work. I put my fist through a wall. (No, really, I did. It was in that season of life that I learned the fine art of drywall repair! But I digress.)

He did lots of sleeping. I did lots of yelling. Basically, I remember feeling like a single mom raising three kids in hell, so at one point I packed my bags and prepared to leave. For good.

Then one day, in the middle of a fight, we just stopped. Somehow we mutually decided we were worth too much to throw it all away. But it certainly couldn't stay the way it was. We had to find a way to make it fun again. With the help of counseling and wonderful friends who supported us (and pointed out when we were being idiots to each other), I can honestly say we've done that.

Over the years since then, we've discovered a lot of strategies to keep the fun in our dys-*fun*-ctional family . . . and to celebrate each other, even when life's making us cry.

ACKNOWLEDGE THE ENEMY IN YOUR MARRIAGE (IT'S NOT YOUR SPOUSE)

When frustrated, annoyed, incensed, provoked, bothered, or otherwise stressed by your spouse, it's easy to think the enemy is the one standing in front of you, acting like a nimrod. But really, there's a lot more to this story (beyond that it takes one to know one, as we discussed in the last chapter). We've discussed some of what your spouse is going through—and the internal stress, pain, and grief these issues bring to your interactions. Recalling that in a tense moment gets us halfway to "my spouse is not the enemy." What gets us the rest of the way, and turns us back in the direction of joy, is recalling 1 Peter 5:8, where Paul says, "Be sober-minded; be watchful. Your adversary the devil prowls around like a roaring lion, seeking someone to devour" (ESV). We are not alone in those friction-riddled moments with our spouses. In fact, we never are.

There *is* a battle going on, but our pieces of the stress pie are mere slivers of it. In his book *Waking the Dead: The Glory of a Heart Fully Alive*, author John Eldredge reminds us of the context in which we're living. He writes, "War is not just one among many themes in the Bible. It is *the* backdrop for the whole Story, the context for everything else. God is at war. He is trampling out the vineyards where the grapes of wrath are stored. And what is he fighting for? Our freedom and restoration."[1] God's enemy—and hence our enemy—is fighting back, and he'll use whatever foothold we give him to win the bigger battle that rages. Let's not make it easier on him by holding on to resentment with our spouses!

GET AWAY TOGETHER

Get out of town with your spouse, or at least out of the house. Have a regular date night that gets canceled only if someone's in the ER. We've stuck with this even during the years when my husband was starting his business (a.k.a. we were living on a shoestring and our kids were on the free lunch program at school). Where there's a will, there's a way, and this way is one worth fighting—and budgeting—for.

Beyond making time for each other, when you can trust you'll be able to have a conversation (or at least go to the supermarket together, unaccompanied by kids), plan occasional double dates with another couple you enjoy. This has been a huge gift for us on the weeks we can barely think straight with all that the family's going through. It takes the pressure off the two of us to make conversation, and it refreshes us as we engage the other couple's perspective and personalities.

Also, even if it seems as though this would be impossible, plan to get away every once in a while for at least twenty-four hours. Discount travel websites like Priceline.com make it really reasonable. And online caregiver sites like Care.com can help you find a trained respite provider so that when you do get away you can actually let yourself—mind, body, heart, and soul—get . . . away.

CARVE OUT SAFE EMOTIONAL SPACES AS A COUPLE

Get counseling or coaching or meet with a pastor or other person you both trust. Whatever you do, find a space that gives you a safe place to fight, reconnect, and heal *together* instead of growing apart. On the same topic, censor ignorant marital advice (i.e., ignore naysayers). Surround yourself with people who value your marriage as much as you do, and graciously decline input from those who don't.

Find a space that gives you
a safe place to fight, reconnect,
and heal *together* instead of
growing apart.

Outside of meeting with your safe people, create an emotionally open and safe place for each other at home. Every once in a while (we do it about once a month) ask each other how you see the marriage. Four questions that have helped my husband and me stay connected are:

What do you want me to do more of?
What do you want me to do less of?
What do you want me to start doing?
What do you want me to stop doing?

Never assume you know each other's minds completely; even if you did, people grow and change (we want that, even if it's a little more work for us, right?). It honors our spouses when we give them space to change and become more of who God designed them to be, and it honors our marriages when we invest in that safe space ourselves.

STOP BEING A KNOW-IT-ALL

Hartley Steiner, author and founder of SPD Network, wrote a post a few years ago titled "Marriage Advice Moms Don't Want to Hear." In it she dishes out a little tough love to us moms, and at one point she shares her perspective on why we can be so hard on dads:

> What often happens during the never-to-be-quenched-thirst-for-knowledge-mission [after a child's diagnosis] is a polarization between husband and wife. You cop an "I know the answers" attitude that quickly leaves your husband to play the role of "guy who doesn't know the answers." And about a year or so down the road, you turn around and realize that YOU have done ALL of the work. And you get angry. Frustrated. Annoyed . . . that your husband doesn't understand your child or appreciate all that you do. Sound familiar?[2]

Um, yes. It does.

What's Hartley's recommendation? "Reconnect with your hubby and remind him of the girl he married—the younger, less stressed, less controlling, less 'OMG DON'T DO THAT WITH THE KIDS!' version of you—remember her?"[3] Easier said than done. But still doable. How?

When you want to criticize, don't. For at least ten full seconds, just breathe and observe. Hold that tongue. You may be surprised at how well what your spouse is doing will work. And you'll certainly discover what author Elizabeth Gilbert shares in her book *Committed: A Skeptic Makes Peace with Marriage*: "You can measure the happiness of a marriage by the number of scars that each partner carries on their tongues, earned from years of biting back angry words."[4]

When you feel you need to give your spouse feedback—he or she didn't harm the child, but the strategy isn't ultimately as helpful or therapeutic as the technique you use—bring it up afterward. Use the sandwich technique, a strategy that, according to Dr. Anne Dohrenwend, director of Behavioral Medicine in Internal Medicine at McLaren Regional Medical Center, "consists of one specific criticism 'sandwiched' between two specific praises."[5] By offering feedback this way, we show our spouses that we value their strengths, recognize their effort, and respect them enough to be honest and open in our joint parenting effort—three ingredients that rekindle joy in our marriages.

SCHEDULE TIME TOGETHER . . . DURING THE DAY

There's only so much energy to go around, and the likelihood of any of it still being around in the evening is, well, *not* likely. How do we ensure that our spouses don't end up with the dregs of our time and attention? By tithing. Many of us tithe (donate some percentage off the top from our paychecks) to charities or our churches to demonstrate that we trust and honor God first. We can use the same idea to tithe some of the first moments or best times of day to our spouses to show them they're important to us too.

Relationship specialist Dr. Laura Marshak, coauthor of *Married with Special-Needs Children*, asserts, "If you spent a mindful 20 minutes a day on your marriage, the impact would be considerable and this would still be less than 2 percent of your day."[6] With all we're managing we might want to protest, "But I don't even have twenty minutes a day!" My response? Start small: twenty minutes one day a week. Then build it up to two days a week for a few weeks, and keep going until it becomes a daily routine.

As a coach and author I work from home much of the time, but my husband's job has him working all over the place. When he has seasons working from home, we plan (or notice and capitalize on) pockets of mid-morning time to hang out while both of us are still alert and fresh. When he works outside the house we plan to get up earlier than the kids for some together time before the daily chaos ensues. When that hasn't been possible during different seasons of our family life, we institute the "I only have eyes for you" rule: for the first ninety seconds we interact after not seeing each other for a few hours, we hug, look at each other, and let life's—and the kids'—demands take a backseat.

GIVE YOUR SPOUSE THE BENEFIT OF THE DOUBT

Feedback can be one of the toughest, most stressful aspects for a couple raising a child with special needs. But then again, it's communication, and that's tough in any marriage. The difference between the marriage that survives challenging discussions and the one that doesn't is in large part in how we approach the conversations.

Dr. John Gottman of the Gottman Institute has dedicated his research to studying what makes and breaks married couples. He says, "The way couples begin a discussion about a problem—how you present an issue and how your partner responds to you—is absolutely critical."[7] Couples who enter a conversation assuming the best of the other person enjoy longer, more fulfilling marriages. The Gottman Institute reports that "volatile couples can stick together . . . when their disagreements are had in a state of Positive Sentiment Override."[8] Positive Sentiment Override (PSO) is described very clinically on Gottman's website, but it boils down to this: what's your default perspective of your spouse?[9] Do you choose to believe the best about him? Or do you skew toward hearing her words and seeing her behavior through a negative lens? If you tend to be glass-half-full (as opposed to half empty) in terms of your outlook on your spouse (which is a choice we can make, moment by moment), you're well on your way to joy in the marriage.

Couples who enter a conversation assuming the best of the other person enjoy longer, more fulfilling marriages.

DON'T EXPECT YOUR SPOUSE TO MEET ALL YOUR NEEDS

Not only do lasting, fulfilled couples have good communication, but they do what they can to take care of the needs over which they don't see eye to eye. We can give positive, sandwich feedback all we want, but if our spouses don't agree a change is necessary, or they simply can't make that change right now, we can still take care of ourselves and the non-negotiables our kids need.

For example, my husband and I argued for years about my wanting him to help more around the house. I shared the need in a feedback sandwich: "I really appreciated you helping to put the kids to bed tonight. I need your help with the dishes a few nights a week too. You're great with brainstorming, so what could that look like?" I followed up every few weeks, changing the positive examples each time. He would do them one night, commit to doing them more often, but fail to follow through, undercutting my trust and reliance on him as my parenting partner.

One day I decided to stop getting mad, admit that this kind of assistance wasn't his forte, and get what I needed (help with the house) in another way. I found out about federal financial assistance options for families with adoptive kids with special needs like ours, applied to receive that aid, and used the money to hire a part-time sitter/home helper who took care of what my husband wouldn't/couldn't/didn't. It ended that resentment issue between us because what I really needed was to have an extra set of hands—they didn't need to be his. Doing the work of forgiving him for the ways he'd let me down helped us get back to that Positive Sentiment Override mode, and choosing to let him not be the end-all-be-all of meeting my needs made space for the hurt to yield to joy.

DON'T UNDERESTIMATE THE IMPORTANCE OF SEX

Really. It doesn't have to be a big rose-petals-on-the-bed deal every time—it just needs to be a priority. When I've fought this, thinking (as women often do), "I don't feel like it," guess what? The feeling rarely returns on its own. You've heard some of my story and about the kids we have. Would *you* feel in the mood after days like that? At some point my husband and I heard about a church whose pastor challenged married couples to have sex for thirty days in a row. I balked, ranted, and whined that there was no way that would be possible with a family like ours. But trust me, there is a way. And the connection and playfulness intimacy weaves into marriage—especially one with challenges like we've got—are so worth it.

ABOVE ALL ELSE, PRAY FOR YOUR SPOUSE

Above are just some of the strategies that have helped my marriage, as well as many other couples. Whatever strategies you use, make them your own. If you try something that entails a lot of work but makes a big improvement in the marriage, stick with it. Get support to help you do so. Pray hard, asking God to help you stick with it. If you try a strategy that takes concerted effort and find that unwelcome work is all it is, month after month, make a decision: does it make me happier? If yes, then keep it. Does it decrease the stress in the household, even if it's not changing anything with your spouse (yet)? Yes? Keep doing it. Is it making you more tired and just not working for your family? Yes? Drop it like a bad habit.

Whatever you do, whether or not it seems to work, bear in mind that, more than anything else in your marriage, you've got to be praying for your spouse. Pray for their grieving process. Pray for their jobs. Pray over their other relationships. Pray for their parenting strategies to grow and expand. Pray for their peace, and for their lives to overflow with all the fruit of the Spirit.

More than anything else in your
marriage, you've got to be praying
for your spouse.

When we're feeling as though nothing's working and we're a mess (each of us individually, and corporately as a couple) and like it's never going to get better, that's the moment to pick up a resource like the Bible and start praying through Scripture for our marriages and families. That's the moment to crack open that old copy of Stormie Omartian's *The Power of a Praying Wife*, or whatever other resource you bought when you were first married and it was exciting to love your spouse however you possibly could. Remember?

Pray often. Pray honest. Whine, complain, rant, fuss, and gripe at God if you have to. Then take that extra step and, even if you're so upset you're spitting the words, pray for God to bless your spouse, and bless big-time. That's the flash point at which the joy we work so hard to kindle with our other strategies gets fanned into a brilliant flame.

Eight

CAN'T WE ALL JUST GET ALONG?
(FORGIVING EXTENDED FAMILY)

I've heard family explained as being like a bag of trail mix: a combination of sweetness and a whole bunch of nuts. These days families look different from those in years past—we're no longer living and working the fields with extended family. We're lucky if our primary family members—our parents and siblings—live in the same state, let alone right down the street. Beyond that, many of us are raising kids who wouldn't have lived past infancy back when medications, treatments, and technology were less developed. These factors combine to leave us without a historic example of what extended families can be to parents raising kids with special needs.

In that void we set about creating our own versions. Sometimes that goes well, sometimes not. According to what I've heard and read from other parents, following are the areas that breed the most struggle with our parents, siblings, and other extended family members.

WE FEEL BLAMED OR ACCUSED

"My father actually told me that my son would probably attack me less if I was less controlling," admitted Kelly, the mother of a son with ADHD, ODD, SPD, mood disorder NOS, and bladder/bowel dysfunction. She, like others raising kids with "invisible" disabilities, has a child who is a ticking emotional and behavioral time bomb. She knows from experience what ignites a meltdown, but she also knows from experience that she can't predict every sensory, relational, or emotional trigger possible. So she watches closely. Like me with my oldest, she's got one eye on her son, one eye on the rest of life. Waiting to triage a crisis. Because nine times out of ten, there is one. Does that make her—us—controlling? Maybe. But does that mean we're *causing* our kids' challenges, as Kelly's father accused her of doing? Not necessarily.

Half of the survey responders listed extended family as their hardest relationship as the parent of a high needs child and shared comments like hers. The blame implicit in words like these cuts deep. When we're doing all (and beyond!) that we can to raise our children well, blame shakes both our confidence and our sense of worth. If those related to us can mistrust us with regard to our interaction with our own kids, we begin to question not just what we do but our value as parents.

Just as we do, our extended family members have hopes and dreams for us and our kids. Our parents want to see themselves—and younger versions of their own offspring—in the faces of their grandkids. Our siblings want to catch glimpses of their childhood memories with us in our kids. They all want to see our little ones take first steps, celebrate milestones, and anticipate rites of passage. When they discover that our children aren't able to reflect much of them at all (and let's not even get into the issues of heredity, or their not wanting to be in any way responsible for or connected to this young family member's challenges), they find themselves launched into grief. Grief that, like ours, cycles through bargaining which can come out as accusation and blame against us.

While, yes, it is fair to ask family members to give us the benefit of the doubt and be on our teams in this challenging parenting role, that doesn't mean it's going to be *easy* for them to do so. Especially when it comes to disabilities like those with which Kelly's son struggles, it can require a leap of faith for extended family members to believe that a child who can seem so "normal" can behave in such challenging ways. The issue isn't whether they need to believe us, fully understand the issues, or even engage often with our child. It's whether they're willing to support us as people, affirm that we're doing our best, and love us even through what's hard for them to understand. When that doesn't happen we feel judged, abandoned, and hurt.

The issue isn't whether family
members need to fully understand
the issues, or even engage often
with our child. It's whether they're
willing to support us as people
and love us.

WE FEEL QUESTIONED OR MISUNDERSTOOD

Not as overt a reaction as blame, but no less painful, many parents report feeling unsupported by extended family because rather than encouraging, family members question the choices they make in raising and caring for their special kids. Amy, the mom of a daughter with PDD NOS, expressive/receptive speech disorder, and bowel dysfunction explained it this way: "Half of our family is super supportive, the other half (mainly my siblings) are anything but supportive. One is a nurse who lives thousands of miles away, another one works with older children with autism in a school setting—also lives thousands of miles away—and both have 'other opinions' about this child they barely ever see."

First, let's not overlook that first half of Amy's family. Noticing and celebrating these positive relationships is crucial to our joy, and we'll dig into that in the next chapter. But before we do, let's take a moment to unpack the other half she mentioned, because there's a theme here that came up in more than one parent interview I conducted: it isn't the uninformed family members who question our decisions but often the ones who *do* know something about our children's conditions that can shrivel our confidence as primary caregivers.

To this I can add personal experience with my sister, who is a registered nurse. As a sister, she's one of my favorite people in the world. She's spunky, funny, loyal, and deeply devoted to the Lord. As a nurse, she's intuitive, creative, great with patients, and she's responsible for innovating the health programs at the school where she works. Professionally, she knows about a lot of medical, behavioral, and psychiatric conditions and their current treatment theories and practices. As a sister, she's seen what some of those conditions look like at home in a family—my family. When the two roles mix, and I've called to talk to my *sister*, but the *nurse* in her wants to suggest behavioral or developmental therapies along the line of many others I've tried, I want to shut down or throw the phone.

My brain tells me my sister wants the best for her nieces and that she has professional wisdom to share. But my heart hurts and says, "She knows the lengths to which we've gone to care for our girls. However she intends her suggestions, I'm feeling discouraged right now. I need my sister to listen to and support me. I need to know from her—one of the people I love most in the world—that I'm going to survive this. Somehow."

The good news is that in those moments I can simply say, "I need my sister right now. Let's talk about those therapeutic ideas later," and she responds with grace and acceptance. In that, I'm incredibly blessed. Not all parents surveyed share the same positive interactions. Some feel their families question or suggest ideas because it's uncomfortable to watch them parent their intense or highly fragile children. We're wired as people to reject discomfort, so that's not so hard to understand. But the questioning and not seeking to understand parents' deeper needs as family members leaves many feeling insecure and unsupported by those they need most.

WE FEEL ISOLATED OR LEFT OUT

Isolation can happen for lots of reasons. Sometimes intentionally, as was the case with Ann, the mother of two now-grown sons diagnosed as kids with autism. She explains, "Many members of my extended family refused to believe that my kids had autism. And some siblings excluded us from family activities." Ann's isolation was due to her family's decision to stop including her and her kids.

Some isolation isn't direct or complete like that. It's more like a glass ceiling—we bump up against it in certain situations. In my case, it's with my mom. After my two older girls moved in as foster kids, she made it a point to come from another state to visit every month for the first year.

Upon her arrival she'd swoop in to take care of me like the helpless child I felt myself to be, until days later when she'd fly back home (and, presumably, sleep for a week since she'd worked so hard to be my respite!). Years later she still rallies when I need her. In fact, she sat with me for hundreds of hours while I wrote this book, praying for me and for these words.

I didn't know it when the girls were toddlers, but I'd imagined that same level of support would always be there from my mom. As much as she's earned sainthood, there's a glass ceiling for me that leads to a feeling of isolation. My older two girls are bigger now and that's brought limits on how much my mom feels comfortable helping me with them. It makes sense, really, since I haven't always conveyed a huge level of confidence with the older two. I've shared the good, the bad, and the ugly, and admittedly in recent years (at least with respect to one of them) we've been heavier on the last two topics. But that doesn't make it less painful when she says she's sorry but she just doesn't feel as though she can watch all my kids at once or have our child with enuresis stay at her house, even if we stock her up with encouragement and the supplies our daughter will need.

Do I fault her for that? No. As with my sister, *my brain* knows it's intense to care for my kids even at my age, let alone for my mom in her sixties. I understand that, even with "normal" kids, four kids are a lot to manage! I understand her desire not to have to deal with enuretic accidents in her home, after all, I don't want them in mine either. But in my heart . . . that's another issue. I *feel* left out, isolated from having what my sister or brother has with her: the ability to simply call and ask her to watch their kids—*any of their kids*—when they want her help. I resent that she can set a limit I wish I could set but can't. She can say no to watching my kids; God hasn't given me that option.

Even writing this, I feel embarrassed to share the truth of this struggle. It sounds so immature, so whiny. I'm not alone in those feelings, though. A fellow writer, Lena, blogged about two friends of hers who'd become isolated from their extended families because of both the kids' limits and these parents' desire not to rock the boat: "Both of these people were married, both have young children, both have a child with special needs, both have the weight of the world on their shoulders, and both of them felt that they could not talk to their loved ones for fear of causing more stress for them. These two wonderful, loving, caring, and amazing individuals were lonely, though not alone."[1]

This is something we've all felt in some way. This "other-ness," this sense that we don't really belong or fit in the family, whether or not we've been told as much. The "culprit" may be the direct actions of family members or it may simply be our feelings—feelings which don't follow our chronological age or what we know in our minds to be the truth. In either case, admitting the true nature of our feelings of isolation is the beginning of finding the freedom and joy for which we long with our extended families.

WE MIGHT EVEN FEEL ABANDONED

No matter how old we are, no matter how well our families of origin have gotten along, deep down we long for our families to support us unconditionally . . . and forever. To include us, even if we ourselves or our kids are high maintenance. To treat us as though they're on our team, even if they don't understand why we parent the way we do or why our kids don't progress according to traditional models of development. We expect them to be as up to the task of loving us and our kids as our circumstances require us to be. When they can't or won't fill that expectation, at the very least we can feel emotionally abandoned.

It may not be that they're snubbing us or giving us direct reasons for feeling hurt; instead they may be revealing indifference, disregard for the struggles we face. They may not call, or if they do the conversations may be all about them and their situations. Maybe this is because they don't know what to say or don't want to hear what, to them, may sound like excuses for our kids' challenges. Maybe they would have acted like that about our kids even if our daughters were Olympic athletes or one had become president of the United States. Whatever the reason, the not asking—the issue skirting—hurts almost as badly as the direct criticism.

Beyond this seeming disinterest in our situations, family members may take it further by ceasing to offer help of any kind. This absence of nurturing—which we construe as neglect—represents broken promises to us. As one mom reflected in my survey, she isn't looking for her family's time for respite every week (although that would be amazing); what she wants is "just their support." To listen to her, to be there in spirit even if they can't be there in person. The lack of this emotional backup serves only to underscore the sense we already fight back in ourselves that we're not important, that our experiences don't matter, or that our pain isn't real. That it's really only our kids who matter—not the people taking care of them, their invisible parents.

WHY THE FAMILY WOUNDS HURT DEEPLY

Our brains are built on interpersonal connection. From infancy our neurobiology (the structure and function of our brains) was built through connection with the people researchers call our "attachment relationships." Such persons—whether mother, father, grandmother, aunt, sibling, or other caregiver—were the ones to whom we looked for safety, reassurance, comfort, strength, and a sense that no matter what we'd be okay. For many of us, it was our moms who filled this significant role. They played with us, exchanged smiles, laughed with us, and disciplined us. Through those small but frequent interactions, they gave us a sense of who we are and what the world is all about. Our minds were developed in relationship with these primary attachment figures—those people who meant the most to us and cared for us the most.

Attachment is serious stuff. And that's why it hurts so deeply to have our families of origin and extended family members reject our pain directly in their words and actions, or indirectly by neglecting to support us in the challenges we face. It's a betrayal—whether they intend it that way or not—and our brains feel as though a hurricane has ripped through us, laying waste our relationships, our emotional landscape, and our basic understanding of the world.

If you just read those last two paragraphs and thought to yourself, "Great, I'm already screwed, because things weren't so safe, comforting, healthy, or loving for me as a kid with my parents," don't worry. Even if your family history was riddled with dysfunction, it's likely that someone else in your life filled that attachment role. As a character in Jim

Butcher's novel *Proven Guilty* states, "I don't care about whose DNA has recombined with whose. When everything goes to hell, the people who stand by you without flinching—they are your family."[2]

Someone, somewhere along the line, became an attachment figure to you. Maybe it was a teacher, a sibling, someone further out on a limb of the family tree, a neighbor, a counselor, a pastor, or a youth leader. Whoever it was, whoever filled that need in your situation, it's on the basis of that relationship that the forgiveness techniques and the joy-restoring ideas that follow can bring healing and relief.

PRACTICING FORGIVING EXTENDED FAMILY

- Family is trail mix, plain and simple. As Marjorie Pay Hinckley is quoted as saying, "Home is where you are loved the most and act the worst."[3] Many of our extended family members have known us since we were kids. Perhaps when tough interactions punctuate our days, we can picture ourselves as the awkward ten-year-olds they remember—testing limits and fibbing our way out of consequences—and try to take ourselves as seriously as we're now asking our families to do. This doesn't prevent the sting of fresh hurts, but it does give larger context to today's struggles, making forgiveness less impossible.

- We're all part of the nutty and the sweet in the mix. It's not as though we've never given them a dose of judgment, unsolicited advice, or criticism (if you haven't, I need you to mentor me in this regard). When we feel neglected, rejected, or abandoned, we do well to take a deep breath and a long look at ourselves in the mirror—at our own unrealistic expectations, sense of entitlement, and good old-fashioned dysfunctional family behavior over the years. This helps us remember that we're all sorely in need of grace and makes it easier for us in turn to give it to our families.

Nine

REGAINING JOY IN YOUR FAMILY

"There's no such thing as a perfect family."
—Elisa Morgan, *The Beauty of Broken*

The last chapter took me about three times as long as the others to write. Mostly because I've been blessed beyond measure by the ways in which my family has surrounded and supported me in parenting my kids—they haven't given me much to work with in terms of needing forgiveness. And also because we've worked hard over the years to get to this good place as a family. So why would I bring up old hurts—even little ones?

Why take the risk of rocking the family boat? Because a little shaking up provides just enough counterpoint to reveal the vast good that's been my experience, to highlight what many parents have shared as joy-builders in their extended families, and to encourage us to revel in the life-giving truth implied in Elisa Morgan's statement, "There's no such thing as a perfect family."

BE INVOLVED IN THEIR LIVES

When I asked my mom what she has seen me do that has made joy possible in our extended family, the first thing she said was, "You're involved with them [my sister and brother] and their kids." I thought about that for a moment and realized that it makes sense. People don't care how much we know unless they know how much we care, right? If I want my extended family to be involved with me or my kids, I need to do what I can to invest in their lives too. What's that like in our family? Definitely not hour-by-hour involvement, that's for sure. It's a mish-mash of watching my nieces for a day, texting my sister to say "hi" while she's at work, calling my brother when I think of him, or getting together with my mom and asking her how her new Bible study is going.

It's about remembering that while this parenting role I've got is more than I ever expected, my family of origin is still important. It's giving them some priority in the small moments I can scrounge up here and there. It's taking care of myself enough that I have some "me" left over for them and for others I care about. It's about remembering that we're to love others as we love ourselves . . . the second great commandment Jesus gave us during His time on earth (see Matthew 22:37–40). When we make an effort—small though it may be—we open a door to the joyful exchange of effort on both sides.

NOTICE THEIR EFFORTS

It's easy to get stuck on the negative things, isn't it? Our minds are actually wired that way—to give more weight to the negative than the positive memories and emotions. Perhaps that's a neurological leftover from centuries past, when it was important to our daily survival to notice and evade danger (associated with negative or alarming experiences or information). Whatever the reason, we all suffer from negativity bias, this tendency to be influenced more by the negative than the positive.

This innate tendency inadvertently leads us to less joy and positivity in our extended family relationships. *Psychology Today*'s Hara Estroff Marano shares the details: "Occasional big positive experiences—say, a birthday bash—are nice. But they don't make the necessary impact on our brain to override the tilt to negativity. It takes frequent small positive experiences to tip the scales toward happiness."[1]

Frequent positive experiences. That phrase may make your heart sink if you haven't historically had those with your extended family. But the good news is this: gratitude creates positive experiences. When the apostle Paul encourages us to "give thanks in all circumstances; for this is

God's will for you in Christ Jesus" (1 Thessalonians 5:18), it's for a reason: so we can live the abundant life. Gratitude in all circumstances—in each circumstance in which extended family members offer support, attempt comfort, or show up for us in any way—changes our experience of the situation. It points to what's good, right, and special in those moments. It points to grace and hope and love. As we notice and quietly (or audibly) give thanks for the good, we create memories weighted in that direction, growing our experience of joy in our families.

Gratitude in all circumstances—
in each circumstance in which
extended family members offer
support, attempt comfort, or show
up for us in any way—changes our
experience of the situation.

INVITE THEM INTO YOUR WORLD

If traditional moments like birthdays and holidays are uncomfortable, intersperse them with the nontraditional ones that make up your life as a parent of special kids. Invite family members to the urology appointment where your ten-year-old will graduate from wearing daytime pull-ups. Include them in the exit visit when you bring your child home from the hospital after that long round of treatments.

We discovered this idea during the eighteen months our second daughter was in a local residential treatment facility. I remember planning to get together with my sister, brother, and parents on a day when we needed to go and visit our daughter. One of them offered to come with us—after which all of them jumped on board. We might have said, "No, that's okay. It's intense there, and it may be weird or even a little scary for the younger cousins." We could have said we'd visit our daughter first and then meet up with everyone else afterward. In short, we could have kept them at arm's length rather than opening the can of worms that was our family situation that year—complete with our psychiatrically unstable daughter and about a hundred other troubled kids whose screams were audible down hallways and as we walked the premises. But we let them in. We invited them to be part of the weird that was us during that year and a half. And in a show of enormous love and acceptance on their part, they came.

What indescribable joy to have them there! I had no idea how hard it would be for me that year. How dislocated I'd feel emotionally and mentally, trying to grapple with questions like, "Will she ever be okay again?" "Will she ever be able to come home?" and "Do I want her to if she can?"

That was one of the toughest years I've had raising this child, and simply including family made it livable. More than that. It opened the door for a whole new set of memories to be made, strange and chaotic as they were. Might they have declined the invitation? Yes. They could have ignored and even shunned us. They could have freaked out and left us floundering on our own. Sometimes that happens in families. But what they might have done wasn't within our control—the invitation was. If we'd never asked (or, in this case, acquiesced to a gracious offer), we may have saved ourselves from potential rejection, but we'd have lost some precious bonding moments too.

Someone once put it this way: If you never ask, you never have to hear them say no, but you'll certainly never hear them say yes. So keep asking. Keep inviting. Who knows what joy that could usher into your relationships with your extended family?

HELP FAMILY HELP YOU

This strategy comes easily to us as parents since we're ready and willing to help people better understand our kids and know how to help and relate with them well. But can we communicate that with family members in a way that still allows them to *be family* (as opposed to those, albeit invaluable, paid respite care workers or professionals on our child's treatment team)?

When I asked my family members what gives them the most joy in their interactions with my kids, my mom responded that she's felt empowered to relate with them—even in the harder seasons we've faced—once I've explained the world through their eyes. In our case that means sharing what I've learned about adoption attachment, the girls' mental health challenges, ADHD and PTSD, and what these conditions look like in different situations. Instead of arming my family with a list of strategies to use (though I've been advised to do that too), the real benefit is to help them understand my kids from the inside out.

Encouraging and sharing the children's perspective does two things: it fosters the connection between my kids and our extended family, and it prepares our family for anything out of the ordinary they may face with our girls. It makes interacting with our daughters less about their needs and more about the family relationships and bonds that are possible. In other words, it invites the family—the whole family—to become part of our new normal, instead of emphasizing what they don't understand and what's different about us.

ASSIGN SOMEONE ELSE TO THE JOB OF AFFIRMING YOUR WORTH

June Hunt, biblical counselor and popular radio show host, writes, "If your sense of self-worth is based on the approval of others, you are on a runaway roller coaster with no ability to control when you are up or down. Your feeling of value is at the mercy of what others think about you."[2] Any time we look to anyone, family or otherwise, to define and affirm us, we're in for trouble. The Bible says that "the human heart is the most deceitful of all things, and desperately wicked. Who really knows how bad it is?" (Jeremiah 17:9 NLT). And that includes the hearts of even the people closest to us. Why would we use that as a mirror if it's reflecting hurt and shame to us?

Thus the first step in forgiving family is to remember that while their thoughts and opinions are some of the most important in our lives, they aren't flawless beings. The only person off whom we can with confidence bounce our identity is the One who created us—the God who made us in His image and who is the only family member we can trust implicitly. That's because He is holy (righteous, pure), good, and the embodiment of love (Joshua 24:19; Psalm 136:1; and 1 John 4:8).

The God who made us in
His image is the only
family member we can
trust implicitly.

If we're doing what we know to be right for our kids, are open to feedback, and are seeking God's heart and ways as parents, we can rest in the truth that no matter how our family responds, "if God is for us, who can be against us?" (Romans 8:31). We can take the gavel out of our family's hands and give it back to the One who can truly see—and caringly deal with—us and our situation.

SOAK YOUR MIND IN THE TRUTH

Once we've reframed the weight we assign to the responses of our extended family members, we continue to release ourselves from resentment by grabbing hold of the truth. This takes work, yes. We'll keep wishing we could lean on our family for strength and a sense of personal worth. This may never happen, and for that we need to let ourselves grieve—to be mad, be sad, make bargains, be indifferent—and then let it go.

Scripture can help with each place in which we find ourselves. It can become the personal guidance system we crave through family, our affirmation in the day-to-day steps of faith we take, our comfort as we flip out when it all gets hard. Sometimes it takes a change of pace or strategy in our deepest relationships to shake us up a little and invite fresh trust in the truth of God's Word.

Linda Breitman, mentor and author of *The Real You: Believing Your True Identity*, recommends posturing ourselves in God's view of us through Scripture: "When you posture in God's Word, you position yourself to be in agreement with God. . . . You are aligning yourself with God's perspective. . . . You take up the sword of the Spirit which is the Word of God and proclaim it."[3] As it relates to our relationships with extended family, posturing can look like this:

I feel abandoned. But you, God, will never leave me or forsake me (see Hebrews 13:5).

I feel rejected. But you, God, fully accept me as your child (see John 1:12).

I feel misunderstood. But you, God, know my deepest thoughts (see Psalm 139:1–5).

Breitman writes, "Our concept of self worth is based on our believing our identity. As we know who we are in God's heart, we find true value and self worth."[4] Posturing—orienting our thoughts and perspective—in the truth of Scripture is a huge step toward freedom in our relationships with extended family.

RECONCILE EVEN IF THEY WON'T OR CAN'T

If forgiveness brings peace and freedom, reconciliation seals the deal and marinates it with joy. My friend Suzie Eller, author of *The Unburdened Heart*, shares that through "kaphar forgiveness" extended toward those who have wronged us, "the burden of unforgiveness is released, that burden that we carried even after their death, or if they've continued in their behavior, or if you've had to shut the door to a relationship to stay safe or keep your babies safe, is let loose so we can live in the present."[5]

This shade of forgiveness is what we can call into action when, no matter what we try, interacting with extended family members isn't possible or beneficial. Perhaps they've repeatedly shunned your child, your efforts, your feelings, and the truth of what your family is going through. Perhaps, after confronting, attempting to move past a hurt, and revisiting it again and again . . . it just isn't an option to continue to engage that family member. Joy—not the fleeting feeling that depends on circumstances, but deep, strength-imbuing joy from God—is possible even when relationships can't continue.

As Suzie explains, "Reconciliation doesn't always mean a one-to-one personal encounter. It can mean 'coming to an understanding,' even if no one else signs up."[6] We can be reconciled *about* a relationship without being reconciled *in* it. This isn't ideal. Not what we've wished or hoped for in our extended families. But if the truth is that the relationships bring pain in continuous waves, we can trust God with our families and let Him be to us what they cannot.

Ten

WHEN THE PROS DON'T KNOW (FORGIVING THE PROFESSIONALS)

"I feel constantly buried in the world of kids, medicine, appointments, etc."
—Vicki, mother of a child with brain damage

If you've had a child with special needs for any length of time, you've discovered the joys of a waiting room. As far as I can tell, the only redemptive feature of hours and hours in doctors' waiting rooms is the abundance of fun magazines. Okay, maybe more like a handful of worn, outdated family magazines. But, to their credit, at least they offer some "Oh, I haven't tried that one before" snack-making ideas, and sometimes have interesting quizzes in them as well.

Which is why, after one particularly frustrating pediatric neurology appointment, I found myself thinking about our experience in quiz form. How would you answer these four questions?

When you tell the neurologist that your fourth grader nearly drowned recently during what looked like a seizure, and he instead dwells on her history of post-adoptive behavior struggles, you:

1. Repeat your concern. Perhaps he didn't hear the part about how she lost consciousness and almost drowned in the jacuzzi.

2. Stand up and walk out of the room, because you're tired of wasting time with professionals who don't listen.
3. Ignore his conversational direction and ask what next steps you can take to rule out seizures.
4. Tweet a scathing review of the doctor so anyone listening will know how frustrated you are.

(My answer: 1 and 3.)

When you continue to describe your child's suspected seizures as marked by disorganized, repetitive movements and slurred speech, report that you can't get her attention even when you hold her face in your hands, and he suggests pinching her next time, on the premise that she might be simply daydreaming, you:

1. Repeat your concern. Maybe he didn't hear the part about how she nearly drowned.
2. Stand up and leave, because . . . seriously? Do daydreaming ten-year-olds often have this issue?
3. Ignore his conversational direction and ask what next steps you can take to rule out seizures.
4. Tweet *and* update Facebook friends with a scathing review of the doctor.

(My answer: 1 and 3. And I handed my phone to my child so I wouldn't do 4.)

When you tell this doctor that the psychiatrist referred you because no attention-deficit, mood-stabilizing, or anxiety-treating medications have managed your child's space-out moments, and he says, "Maybe it's time to try ADHD medications?" you:

1. Repeat your concern. He obviously didn't hear the part about how she nearly drowned. Or the part about how you already tried many ADHD medications, to no effect.
2. Stand up and walk out, because . . . now it's some alien, meds-resistant form of ADHD?

3. Ignore his conversational direction and ask what next steps you can take to rule out seizures.
4. Tweet and Facebook update your friends. And blog a scathing review of the doctor.

> (My answer: 1 and 3. I deep breathed so I wouldn't do 2 after waiting three months for this appointment.)

At the end of the visit, the doctor says to come back in six months and asks if you have any questions. You say, "Should I let her go swimming? Or take a bath? What if this happens again?" When he then prescribes a forty-eight-hour Digitrace ("walking" EEG), you:

1. Smile and thank God that the doctor, if not a great listener, at least appreciates the scariness of ignoring the symptoms in your child.
2. Leave the office, crank the music, and have a dance party in your car because you didn't act like the angry mama bear you felt like in there.
3. Thank God that He really is advocating for your child, even if it didn't seem like it for most of the appointment.

> (My answer: all of the above.
> And get frozen yogurt.
> And tell God I'm sorry for not trusting Him.
> Again.)

That visit really did happen. It was not by any stretch the first time my daughters and I had a doctor visit like that. My daughter *did* turn out to have a real seizure disorder. While it may seem silly for me to fashion this into a magazine-esque quiz, it reveals some of the biggest challenges we face with medical and therapeutic professionals treating our kids.

With so many of us having children whose special needs extend into multiple areas of development and disability, we may end up in doctors' and therapists' offices dozens of hours or more even within a given week, possibly doing this for years on end. Is it any wonder that there's opportunity for stress and resentment to build in the relationships we have with our children's treatment professionals?

WE FEEL PUT DOWN

It was probably pretty easy to read this feeling into my quiz above. It's the sense we get from clinicians or educators—not stated, but implied through actions (or inaction)—that we, as parents, are not knowledgeable about our own children's needs or reliable observers of their symptoms. Mary, the mother of a prematurely-born daughter who has hydrocephalus, cerebral palsy, and developmental delays, says, "[Working with professionals] is stressful because many of [them] do not listen when you try to tell them what you think is happening, or that what they want to do will not work. It is frustrating when they think they know better than you do what is best for your child."

I second that opinion. Hundreds of other parents I've talked with over the years would third it (if that's even a term). It's hard enough to parent children with challenging medical, emotional, or developmental issues without professionals questioning our observations and seeming to ignore our input. Or, worse, actually belittling it, as was the case for Rachel, the mother of a nine-year-old with visual impairment and intellectual disabilities. She reflects: "In the past I've felt that they honestly didn't have her best interests in mind (and some of them treated me as if I was the one who didn't). To me, they treated symptoms of her disability and didn't look at the entire, bigger picture, which was frustrating."

While educators, therapists, and doctors don't go into their field intending to disregard their clients' parents, the unintentional effect of their words or actions (or lack of either) is that we become doers—perfectionists, even—who end up doubting our instincts, our feelings, and our design as the parents God appointed for our unique kids.

WE HAVE TO "SPEED DATE" THE PROFESSIONALS

This is a term I coined a few years into the nine-year period of time it took to get my second daughter the help she needed. When so many of our children are passed from one care provider to another in order to establish an accurate diagnosis or treatment, we spend a lot of time trying to bring new professionals up to speed on our children's cases.

The challenge is that not only do we need to provide the important details up front as we meet each new professional, but we also have to convey competence, intelligence, patience, willingness to try new things, and a superhuman level of peace and humor so the professionals won't label us as "that" parent—the one they're inclined to ignore, cut off, put off, or disregard because we're too intense about our child's case. Nina, the mother of a son with Asperger's and PDD NOS, explains what that looked like in a meeting on behalf of her son: "I have had to learn to separate me as Mom with feelings and concerns from the cold hard facts. I have learned they cannot co-exist within IEP and [other] meetings. Quite a struggle . . . as they, the professionals, [seem to be] looking for my 'knee-jerk' reaction so they can blame me for my son's [behaviors]."

While it's reasonable to expect all adults involved in a meeting to discuss a child's care to be professional and polite and to communicate clearly, it doesn't feel reasonable to have to censor our parental feelings or instincts in order to be taken seriously by professionals and get our children the help they need.

It doesn't feel reasonable to have
to censor our parental feelings
or instincts in order to be taken
seriously by professionals and get
our children the help they need.

Beyond that, there's often an added dynamic that one mom of a child with cystic fibrosis explains this way: "[Working with] doctors and specialists who don't [seem to] understand the condition as well as I do is frustrating beyond belief and so stressful, leaving me wondering if I'm doing all I can for my son." Sometimes a professional can seem to understand less about our children's conditions than we do because they are new to the field or our child's case is atypical. In these situations, we as parents find ourselves in a position of needing to convey not only our children's stories but also the basic body of understanding about their needs based on previous specialists' experiences and research. This isn't easy to navigate with a professional who's had decades of combined education and professional experience.

In our daughter's case, this left us in a tough place: we had to come across as respectful, easygoing, and informed while conveying what we already knew did or didn't work (so we didn't waste their time or our own)—a combination that often flew in the face of the respect and easygoing style that the "getting to know you" phase of a relationship calls for. How does a parent emphasize crucial information without seeming inflexible or pushy or entitled? It isn't easy!

WE FEEL LIKE A CHART OR A LABEL, NOT A HUMAN BEING

So many parents I've talked to share stories like ours of having wrapped their schedules around a specialist's availability, taken time off from work, and maybe even planned and paid for childcare for their other children, only to finish their appointment feeling as though the health-care professional didn't hear them or look objectively at what could be contributing to their children's new symptoms or causing issues that have been stubbornly unresponsive to treatment.

We can also feel as though we don't matter when a professional (1) can't get us in to manage a fresh symptom for four months (has happened to us many times); (2) sets an appointment for which we're there ten minutes early, only to have to keep the spinning plates that are our kids balanced in the waiting room for sometimes as long as an hour or more; or (3) calls with no notice to get our children in to an appointment we've been asking about for days. Those kinds of moments leave us feeling as though our children barely matter to the professional involved, and that we parents matter even less.

I remember a particular appointment when my two older girls were preschoolers. We'd made an appointment with a neurologist for my younger one, waited our four months, arrived on time, sat in the waiting room for thirty minutes, moved to the exam room, and sat in there for a full hour before the doctor came in to talk with us. Picture this: a two- and a three-year-old in a ten-by-ten room with nothing but my mom-bag of tricks (markers, coloring books, dolls, snacks, stamps, stickers; this was almost ten years ago, so there weren't any of those ubiquitous smart-phones or iPad happy places yet!). Both girls were potty training, so we had to leave every twenty minutes to use the restroom, which I'd let the receptionist know, concerned that the doctor might see we were gone and move on to another patient.

We missed both kids' nap times, they were hungry, I was hungry, and the stress I felt during that afternoon churned up indigestion, muscle tension, and a headache. Feeling invisible and disrespected will do that to a mom. As will the disappointment of waiting so long to see a profes-sional known as one of the best, only to leave more stressed than you arrived.

WE FEEL OVERWHELMED BY UNREALISTIC EXPECTATIONS

Treatment suggestions, especially of the behavior and mental health variety, are often prescribed and expected at levels that families can't sus-tain over time. They sound good during a ten-minute appointment but run families ragged in practice. Shelly, the mom of a child with ADHD, PTSD, and mental impairment explains, "Doctors sometimes don't real-ize how much stress they put on families. Sometimes their expectations are ridiculous and I have to ask them to put themselves in my shoes and think about, if they actually had to live in my home, how differently they would handle things." Julie, the mom of a teen with global developmental delays, expresses it this way: "The medical community likes to look at a single aspect of a person instead of the person as a whole." This leads to difficulty treating the child and overwhelms the parents trying to admin-ister treatments recommended by multiple professionals, each of whom is trying to treat one isolated facet of their patient's condition.

As a parent of two foster-adopted children, this was always an intense stressor for me. The list of tasks and strategies needed for my older daughters alone—attachment-based parenting techniques, physical ther-apy, speech therapy, occupational therapy, ADHD behavior modification and management strategies, extra learning strategies to help the younger one keep up with peers—filled hours each day. All this with two younger siblings, not to mention my marriage, keeping up the home, and needing to cook for us all . . . just wasn't humanly possible. Even after we received federal adoption assistance to get a trained home helper for twelve to fifteen hours a week, I still wasn't getting to bed at a reasonable hour after all that was needed to care for our girls!

But I don't need to tell you all this. You get it. Your life probably looks a lot like ours, just with different details to cram into the puzzle.

WE HAVE TO MANAGE OUR OWN CARE

How do we manage our own care as we work with the pros? As discussed in the previous chapters, we need to grieve. What does that look like when we're working with professionals who help us care for our kids? It starts with a few basics:

Let yourself feel like a parent.

At the appointments and meetings, listen to your body—where you're keeping your stress, how you're feeling about the interactions you're having with your child's professionals in that moment, and what might help. Before and after the appointments listen to and accept help and support from family members and other people in your life who understand you and your child, who love you intentionally. Both kinds of listening can help in those potentially stressful interactions with the doctors, therapists, educators, and other professionals who help us care for our kids.

We can't stuff it down deep, act as though everything's okay, and smile at doctors when they're recommending something we've already tried many times. Anger ignored develops into depression and resentment. Anger faced, in contrast, loses steam and focuses us on what needs to be done. Be angry about that meeting if you need to, but don't let your rage spill out all over everyone else; you can channel that energy in any direction you choose. That ability is God's gift of self-control in that moment when we feel so helpless. Punch a boxing bag at the gym. Go for a run. Journal like crazy until your hand is tired of writing (that quiz at the beginning of the chapter was one of my journal-and-process-feelings moments). Whatever you do, remember that *you* are in charge of your anger and that you have access to God's own strength to feel and handle it wisely.

Beyond allowing and managing our feelings, we can simply make space in our lives to get through whatever it is we're feeling—whether sadness, anger, weariness, wariness, or anything else. We can plan for a little extra space in those days when we'll see our kids' professionals so we'll have some strength in reserve if it proves to be a tough visit. We can order take-out that night instead of being super parent and cooking from scratch. We can go to sleep a little earlier that night. And we can do all of that without castigating ourselves because we need a little extra TLC.

Let yourself relax during appointments, when you can.

I don't know about you, but my first instinct as my kids lock eyes on the cartoon playing in the doctor's office waiting room is to whip out my phone and work. I'll answer emails; research online for a book, blog post, or client; pay a bill; or return a call to another doctor's office. Not relaxing! And then I wonder why the above issues with my child's professionals get to me as much as they do?

Perhaps you can relate?

Instead of multitasking, what if we let ourselves watch the Disney movie in the waiting room, even if we've seen it a hundred times? Or listened to music on our iPods or phones—music that soothes, adds joy, or helps us get our eyes on God again. We could walk an extra lap up and down the hallway after a bathroom break, just to get moving and be in a different setting (sort of). We could read one of those magazines sitting on the table, nibble on a favorite snack, or put on our favorite smelling hand lotion. If we're artists, we could bring a journal to write or draw, or, if we're organizers, we could clean out and organize our purses or our kids' backpacks. Any of those would relax us and meet emotional needs so we can be the professional we need to be with our child's care team.

Become an even better record-keeper.

You're likely already a pro at keeping track of your child's history of treatments, medications, and anecdotal reports for their team of care professionals. But how well do you document the joy-giving history in and around their care? Make it a point to become a balanced historian in the records you keep. Whether in a journal, blog, by talk-to-text recording as you drive home, or scrawling on a hospital paper towel in the exam room—however you can manage it you owe it to yourself and your child to find a way to see the good stuff.

Record how you felt during those affirming, encouraging, supportive visits—and why you felt that way. Keep those records handy in your purse, in your glove compartment, or on your nightstand to remind you that there has been good in this craziness. Because even for those of us who've experienced instance after instance of difficult meetings with professionals, there are always good moments. We grieve well and live with fuller acceptance and joy when we choose to see and celebrate them as they happen.

PRACTICING FORGIVING THE PROS

- Employ restorative forgiveness. Suzie Eller describes this kind of forgiveness as standing aside and allowing God to intervene. In *The Unburdened Heart* she writes, "With [restorative] forgiveness, you affirm that what happened matters greatly to God, so much that there is an open invitation from God to help you do what you cannot possibly do without His intervention. Over time, with you and God in tandem, He takes that burden."[1] This is frank, swift, this-is-unfair-and-they-don't-deserve-it forgiveness, and it begins with acknowledging the injustice or hurt (such as the time an adoption assistance worker I'd known for nine years had the nerve to accuse me of considering abandonment of my child when I called to brainstorm about a second residential placement) and then aiming it at God to handle. We don't have to muscle through forgiveness. We can trust Paul's pastoral reminder: "Do not take revenge, my dear friends, but leave room for God's wrath, for it is written, 'It is mine to avenge: I will repay,' says the Lord" (Romans 12:19).
- Look at the facts. This forgiveness technique requires no more than a sheet of paper and a pencil. When you're calmer (after you

drive home, after the kids are in bed, over the weekend . . .) write down what happened in the appointment—both the appropriate/ helpful things that were said or done and the inappropriate or hurtful ones. Then make the same kind of list with regard to your own input. If I'm really honest about those hard meetings with professionals over my kids' care, I have to admit that I can get edgy and defensive and convey an air of "it's you against me, buddy," which serves no one, least of all my child. Considering these objective lists of cold, hard facts has helped me more than once to reframe a difficult interaction, acknowledge ways the professional was trying to help, and clarify an issue to be revisited and worked through at the next meeting.

Eleven

RECLAIMING JOY AND CONFIDENCE WITH THE PROS

Barb Dittrich, executive director and founder of Snappin' Ministries, a special needs parents' network, revealed in a blog post recently that even those of us who've been doing this for a while—even those professionally dedicated to helping other parents cope and thrive—struggle with feeling a lack of empathy from professionals. In a post about one of her kids with hemophilia, Barb shares:

> "Bloody noses are just a nuisance," the hematologist proclaimed. I melted into tears and frustrated anger as we stood there in the exam room, sleep deprived and disheveled, lacking a desperately needed shower.
>
> "YOU live with this and see how much of a nuisance this is!" I cried in response. The doctor softened her edge as I buried my face into my hands. She knew it took a great deal to push me to a point where I lose my diplomacy with staff.[1]

In just a few words Barb models one of the best strategies we can use with our kids' professionals: be real with them. Let's look a little more closely at how that works and then consider a few more joy-builders available to us as we interact with the educational, medical, and therapeutic professionals who help our kids.

RECONNECT WITH YOUR INSTINCTS

In the last chapter we noted that one cause for resentment and stress around our child's health-care professionals (or those in any discipline) is feeling as though they don't understand what we observe or experience with our children, or that we don't know what to look for in the first place, even after we've read, researched, and communicated what we're learning regarding their care. We feel stripped of our intuition as parents. Reclaiming joy in this situation begins with learning to trust ourselves again.

My friend Karla shared with me how she reconnected with her instincts as a mom after a harrowing struggle to get help for her son. When he was six weeks old his breathing began to sound a little different. She'd watch his chest when he was lying down, and it seemed as though his breathing was more labored. As he was her second child, she thought he might have simply caught a cold. Over a few weeks she took her son to the doctor a couple of times, and the diagnosis was bronchitis. She followed the treatment plans, only to watch the condition get worse. She ended up at the emergency room six or seven times with him because of his wheezing and coughing, especially when he was lying down. In fact, it got so bad that she would strap him in his car seat so that he would remain sitting upright and be able to breathe more easily.

Visit after visit, doctors assessed her son, gave the diagnosis of bronchitis, and encouraged her to keep up the treatments and return to their office if the symptoms got worse. They always did, and she'd be back in the ER with her infant within a few days. She slept in the same room as her son during this time—"sleep" being a loose term because it was more like night after night of dozing off and then startling awake to check whether her little one was still breathing. On the seventh visit to the ER, as the doctor filled out his chart and declared the problem, yet again, to be bronchitis, Karla looked him in the eye and said, "Listen to me. I'm not going anywhere—I'm not leaving this hospital—until you find out what's wrong with my baby."

Within an hour they'd run the tests that determined her son was allergic to milk. He was choking and having an allergic reaction to the formula he'd been on since six weeks of age, when Karla was no longer able to breastfeed. For six weeks this mom had experienced a mixture of panic, helplessness, exhaustion, frustration, and anger . . . and the resolution and solution required one hour of work on the part of the medical staff. Once she worked through the resentment that experience created, it bolstered her confidence in her parental intuition—a major joy-builder.

BE PREPARED

They say that luck favors the prepared. In my experience joy favors them too. Especially when it comes to our interactions with those in positions of influence with our children's care and education. Jennifer Johnson recommends keeping handy a binder of important information, both for ourselves as a reminder of what we've tried or what our kids have done, and for doctors, so we don't have to reinvent the wheel and spend so much of our "getting to know you" time familiarizing them with our children's cases. Can we ask doctors to be perfect? No. Can we expect them to get it right with our kids about every symptom or challenge they face? No. Can we expect them to listen to us? Yes. And any professional listens more closely when we convey preparedness on our part.

In a blog post Jennifer shared the components of what she keeps in her child's binder:

- A document of bullet points of my son's medical history, including diagnoses (date, who made it), medications (who prescribed, date started, dose), surgeries (dates), hospitalizations (dates), etc.
- Brief developmental status: age equivalent levels for each area (gross motor, fine motor, sensory, social/emotional, speech, etc.); chronological ages he reached developmental milestones (You can find a list of developmental milestones online and then put in the age your child reached each one. I find this one especially helpful when I am overwhelmed with the idea of how far behind we are and don't want to recount it all again. Plus, it saves so much time in meetings.).
- List of names and contact info for all medical providers.
- List of names and contact info for all therapy providers (ABA,

speech, PT, OT, etc.), number of hours of each service per week, who is funding each service.

- Family history form (you can find forms online and fill in your family history info and print out).[2]

A physical binder like this can save a lot of time and, for us as parents, alleviate the pressure of having to convey the situation in a nutshell with 100 percent accuracy. If you're more of a smartphone kind of person, applications like the one at Vestidd.com provide organization and shareability with the rest of your child's care team. My friend and colleague, author Jolene Philo, also wrote a book that gives detailed recommendations, and is soon releasing *The Caregiver's Notebook* as well.[3] Check out her book *Different Dream Parenting* for her great suggestions.[4]

Whatever tool we use, being as prepared as we can helps our visits with the pros—medical, therapeutic, or educational—to be as productive and efficient as possible. A win-win for everyone involved, and a joybuilder for parents balancing as much as we are.

Whatever tool we use, being as
prepared as we can helps our visits
with the pros—medical, therapeutic,
or educational—to be as productive
and efficient as possible.

DOCUMENT YOUR WINS

If preparation like that mentioned above promotes joy and confidence in our interactions with professionals, a cousin to that kind of preparation builds joy in how we see ourselves. The tool I'm suggesting is not simply a list of our questions, the notes we've taken about our children's situations and needs, or the ideas others have suggested, but one we can formulate in our quieter moments. It's a list I like to call, "How I've helped my child so far."

On it we can record as many examples as we can remember of times we've noticed a need and met it; solved a problem regarding our kids' care; followed the quiet internal voice of the Spirit and asked the right question; or made the right change at the right time. My friend Karla's list, from the story above, would include how she noticed a change in her son's breathing, that she caught the issue very early in his life, that she didn't let anyone assure her everything was okay when it wasn't, and that she followed her instincts and took him to the emergency room.

By taking time to listen to the leading of the Spirit, to celebrate the times we've heard Him clearly, and to recognize the common sense we've exercised as parents, we honor the work God has done in and through us thus far. The Bible says that children are a heritage from the Lord. They're given specifically to the parents who have them. We do well to step out and be bold about what we observe in our kids—about their diets, their behavior, their social habits, their sleep and activity habits. To maintain a list of times this has benefited our children helps us retain a sense of confidence that breeds joy in our future interactions with the professionals who help them.

Go ahead. Do it. Take out a piece of paper right now and start to make that list. I guarantee that each line item you add will expand your joy in who God has grown *you* to be as your special child's parent. May it remind you of who you are as a full-fledged member of your child's treatment team. And may that knowledge enhance your meekness—yes, you read that right—that quality of *power under control* both evidenced and touted by Jesus. Our meekness comes from recognizing and acknowledging the power God has cultivated in us. The power of observation, of well-past-the-time-we-used-up-our-energy care, of hope beyond all odds, and of multitasking as we raise our special kids alongside typically developing ones.

For Jesus, meekness looked like listening to and patiently correcting religious leaders who were doing a poor job of understanding and conveying the heart of God (as in the case of misunderstanding the Sabbath and its purpose. See Mark 2:23–27). For us it may look like holding our tongues when a medical or educational professional doesn't seem to be listening, and respectfully sharing our understanding of our child's needs. In either case it's powerful. And making a list of what has gone right in our care of our kids can signal the start of intentional effort to appropriately channel and focus that power.

UNDERSTAND THE SPEED-DATING PROCESS BETTER

While it may not make it easier or more fun for us, we can at least have some solace in knowing that the professionals have to speed date too. A recent article in *Christian Counseling Today* shares what professionals in the mental health field are expected to do with each client. The article reminds practitioners that "treating symptoms without the correct diagnosis can lead to wrong or inadequate treatment and complications."[5] Which means they have to ask all the questions other professionals have already asked so they can do their due diligence and provide the best possible care for our kids.

It's frustrating to answer the same questions over and over. We may not personally be in a place where we're feeling friendly or kind or even remotely interested in meeting yet another person who may or may not be able to help our children any more than the last dozen candidates have. It's tiring and annoying and perhaps at times even more than we can muster the politeness to handle, but the reality is that we've got to do this part. At least until the medical records world gets things more cohesive than is the case right now.

Bear in mind that teachers have certain hoops they must jump through as well. They didn't go into their field bent on making our children's education a painful process. Trust me: as a former public school teacher I can attest to this. Nowhere in the credentialing process do we find advocated a disdain for working with kids with extra challenges. That's not to say every teacher is good at what they do. Ditto for doctors and other medical professionals. But they enter their profession wanting to help people. Medical professionals take an oath in which they commit to doing so, pledging that "the health of my patient will be my first consideration."[6] The realities of health-care reform, medical insurance claims, and our societal tendency to litigious action have all put pressure on those once-idealistic medical and therapeutic students. It isn't our job to reverse what sin and time and society have made of our health and educational systems. But it is our job to advocate for our kids, and joy grows as we keep that goal in the forefront of our minds while meeting and developing relationships with the professionals caring for them.

And I can honestly share from experience that I'm kind of glad I get to present my child afresh to new people. In the neurology appointment I shared in the last chapter, the chart's elaborate recording of my daughter's psychiatric issues and paltry coverage of her medical ones made it hard for the doctor to look objectively at her as a person. She has a legitimate neurological, non-psychiatric seizure condition, and it took the veiled threat of malpractice to get him to treat her as someone who may indeed have medical issues. Having a chance to share her case afresh and convey pertinent details gave me a sense of agency and value in her care. So let's not discount the gift that speed dating can be, especially for our kids who are harder than the average to diagnose and treat!

REFRAME CRITICISM

This is a sticky spot, for sure. We stand in an office with a professional we may have had to seek out and wait for a long time to see and plead our case with, only to face the prospect that they may criticize the way we're handling our children. Especially if the challenges our kids face are resistant to treatment or therapies, a situation I've faced for years with one of my daughters.

As people who value biblical wisdom and maturity, we trust the truth of Scripture that says, "if you listen to constructive criticism, you will be at home among the wise" (Proverbs 15:31 NLT). If we truly want what's best for our kids, we need serious wisdom to raise them well, right? But there's a difference between listening to criticism and allowing it to define us. Author Jon Acuff offers great advice on how to hear criticism without letting it cut us. He recommends that we mentally insert these ten words before processing whatever criticism we may encounter: "I'm a complete stranger with some advice about your life."[7]

How would this look? When the school nurse's aide frowns at you because your daughter refused to drink enough water to manage her encopresis, and you gave her Miralax (per doctor's orders) for a few days to get things moving, which led to her having an embarrassing soiling accident on the playground (after refusing to use the toilet per the health office plan), and the aide says to you, "Your daughter said you did this? Gave her too much Miralax? Maybe you should take her to the doctor [instead of just doing what they said to do] next time she's constipated," I can put Jon Acuff's preamble in front of her I-haven't-read-your-child's-chart-or-attended-any-IEP-meetings criticism. Then it sounds more like this: "I'm a complete stranger with some advice about your life: perhaps you could take her to the doctor next time she's constipated."

Having been the recipient of countless new specialists' criticism of my care for our second daughter, I have to say it's empowering to have this tool. It puts the critique in its proper place: in reality. And it restores our feeling of being respected as fellow—and primary—team members for our kids. When it comes to health-care professionals (or even teachers, nutritionists, or whatever other professionals we're engaging on behalf of our kids), is their feedback important? Yes. Is it well informed? Most of the time. But is it the end-all-be-all for your particular situation and child? No. As a friend and fellow parent-support blogger points out, professionals are well educated about conditions in general, but they're not—nor can they be—experts on that condition *in your child*, because the only expert on what a condition or symptom or side effect does in your child is you.

REJOICE IN THE PROFESSIONALS WHO DON'T TREAT YOU LIKE A CHART

Julie, whom I mentioned in the previous chapter, shares her wish list of what a great interaction for her daughter's treatment would look like: "Real concern and collaboration about helping her reach her potential physically, health-wise, and mentally." If we're honest, all of us have worked with at least one person who's like that with us or our children. Joy comes in our choice to remember those professionals with whom we, or the kids we represent, aren't just a condition, a diagnosis, or a problem. We can thank God for having these people on our teams.

My family has two people on our team like that. The first is a psychiatrist who decided that *he* was where the buck finally stopped for our enigmatic second daughter after we'd bounced from doctor to doctor for years trying to get her help. He makes time to see her even though he has so many patients there's a waiting list for new ones. He listens to me, provides resources, keeps his sense of humor, and thanks me for being a positive piece of the puzzle that comprises my child's life and medical challenges. The second professional who treats our family like, well, *family* is our dentist. He's affable, kind, and the kind of miracle-worker who gets children with Reactive Attachment Disorder to let someone they barely know touch their teeth without a fit. I refer people like crazy to these two professionals. And that was even before I found out recently that dental benefits for my older two ended through their federal program, and our dentist had seen them for free without even bringing up the billing issue for years. (I corrected that when I found out, mind you, because people this good at what they do deserve to be paid as well as is humanly possible!)

When I stand in an office with a provider who doesn't understand me or listen to what my child's experiencing or what I think she needs, I will myself to remember these two amazing practitioners. The ones who actually know me and my child. The ones who've earned my trust and admiration and have helped me hang on when I didn't have anything left.

Who has been that safe, supportive
professional for you or your child?
. . . Whoever it is, spend some time
thanking God for them.

Who has been that safe, supportive professional for you or your child? Is it a teacher? An administrator? A doctor, nurse, or therapist? Whoever it is, spend some time thanking God for them. Send them a thank-you note as well. Write them a great review on Yelp.com or some other site that shares client stories for businesses and institutions.

Refer friends to them. Tell them every time you see them how much they mean to you and your family. Take all that gratitude into your meetings with every single one of your child's professionals. No matter what happens in those meetings, nothing can negate the joy that has come at the hand of the professionals who've been a gift to you and your child.

Why stop at recalling only the professionals who've been a gift? While we're at it, we can boost our joy and confidence in God's own overarching care for our kids and families by cultivating gratitude for every facet of it. Brené Brown, in her book *Daring Greatly*, notes that "if the opposite of scarcity is enough, then practicing gratitude is how we acknowledge that there's enough and that we're enough."[8] When we take the time to acknowledge what's working well and right, not only do our interactions with professionals have a better chance of joy, but every other aspect of our lives does too.

Perhaps that's what the apostle Paul was referring to when he exhorted us to "give thanks in all circumstances; *for this is God's will for you in Christ Jesus*" (1 Thessalonians 5:18, italics mine). If Jesus came "that [we] may have life, and have it to the full" (John 10:10), doesn't it follow that gratitude as described in 1 Thessalonians—in all things, all situations, all struggles—is part of what makes life abundant? As someone who's been raising two children with special needs for a decade, I'll have to admit that I believe it is. When I forget what's good and right in the world, and what God has done to make it so, I see less and less of that goodness and rightness. I go into interactions with my kids' professionals in a defensive instead of a joy-filled stance. I expect to be questioned, belittled, ignored, marginalized, or for my kids to receive substandard care. What good does that do? At best it makes me miserably right if any of those things happen. At worst it sucks away my joy and energy before an outcome can even materialize.

Who needs that extra stress? You don't. Neither do I. So let's be prepared—emotionally and physically. Let's convey meekness, that power under control, and let's walk into those interactions with educational, medical, and therapeutic professionals buoyed by the joy that gratitude can give.

Twelve

LIFE ON THE SIDELINES (FORGIVING CHURCH AND COMMUNITY)

*"In Genesis 3, God said everything was good—
and only called one thing not good: for man to be alone."*
—Lucille Zimmerman, *Renewed*

Kristin and I messaged back and forth one night. It was way past bedtime in her time zone, and I wasn't expecting her to respond when I sent the note that queried, "How are you doing?" after she'd been in and out of the hospital with her child all week. Moments later she responded. Her words were full of the usual—how her child was doing through the ordeal, some choice misunderstandings with medical staff, the fact that she was exhausted—and one sentence that shocked me: "I thought for sure my church would send someone to visit or call to let us know they were praying for us, or send a meal, especially since I'd called to let the pastor know what was going on. Nobody came or even called."

"Unbelievable," I marveled. Especially considering she's so involved with her church and community!

My heart ached for her. She was already exhausted by the week she and her child had endured, but to add disappointment to the mix—to be part of a community with friends who believe in Jesus but don't offer support when it's most needed? Devastating.

Kristin isn't alone in her experience. My colleague and the mother of a young man with autism, Emily Colson shared in a blog post some of the reasons it's hard to engage in community with our kids, especially (and often most heartbreakingly) in our churches:

> The truth is that most families with autistic children can't make it to the door of the church. So our churches don't always see the need. I know, because for many years we were one of these invisible families. Church, like the rest of life, just didn't work. There were barriers, unspoken requirements, like sitting still and staying quiet and paying attention. But there isn't a pause button for autism. Max didn't seem to fit. For five years we stayed home on Sunday mornings. Actually, we stayed home most every other day too, me and my beautiful son, isolated like we were lepers.[1]

And it isn't just families of kids with autism who struggle in this way. Our family has faced the same kinds of challenges with our friends, neighbors, and fellow church members. When our older girls' medications are off and their moods or behaviors skew outside our normal level of chaos, I've canceled everything from shopping errands to their own birthday parties. I've gone to church in the company of my daughters, keeping the older two with my husband and me in the sanctuary so their sisters could attend their classes at church and have a life, wishing every moment I'd just stayed home because it's humiliating to have a kid sitting next to me murmuring and pulling out strands of her own hair the whole time. Our family has opted out of birthday parties for our friends' kids because our daughter has been excluded from other parties based on her challenges, and I don't want to risk our being uninvited or making a scene once again.

Whether or not you're facing similar issues, the kinds of heartaches Emily mentioned, or something like my friend Kristin experienced, as a parent of a high-needs child you've likely faced hurts in the context of community. Friends, neighbors, and fellow church-goers can be a huge support in crisis, and many of us have experienced this many times over! When the crises—the births or adoptions of our special children, or the onsets of new conditions—subside, however, very few communities are able or willing to continue to support struggling families. And is that any wonder? I mean, we ourselves don't feel as though we have it in us to deal with our families' ongoing needs! That said, here are some ways we bump up against hurt in our communities and friendships.

WE FEEL LIKE WE DON'T BELONG AT CHURCH

Of the communities and friendships we've got, it can be the ones associated with our place of worship that result in the most devastating sense of rejection. Kathleen, the mother of two challenged kids, one with muscular dystrophy and the other with autism, seizures, and left-side paralysis, explained, "We moved four years ago. I expected the [new] church to be supportive and include our children . . . [but] that didn't happen." She isn't alone. Rachel, another survey respondent, shared, "We were part of a church who at times treated our daughter as just a misbehaving child throwing temper tantrums and at other times as invisible. It was stressful to have a community who I thought should care the most, not care at all, and I began to hate (and avoid!) going to church."

It's painful to go to a place in which we expect not just to be tolerated but included and accepted, only to find out we're not. Or, sometimes worse, that *some* in our family are not, while others are. Shari explains, "My son with Asperger's is a twin. Everybody at church wanted my daughter in their class, but nobody wanted him." She tried to resolve this, approaching the staff and teachers at her church with her concerns and suggestions for including her son. The more she tried to make it work, the less the church engaged her concerns. "The problem got worse as we took concerns to the church staff," Shari continues. "They seem to have the idea that if they just ignore the problem, it will go away."

Her situation isn't unique, but you probably know that all too well. Perhaps you've approached church volunteers or a pastor to open the dialogue about your child and his needs. Maybe you've educated the staff and other parents whose kids attend church with yours about the special needs they'll encounter as they interact with her. Possibly things started off well—people were willing to include and accommodate your child in nursery or preschool classes and events—but as he grew, the same needs weren't as easily tolerated anymore. You may have even been like one family McLean Bible Church Access ministry leader Jackie Mills-Fernald describes in *Special Families . . . A Casserole's Not Enough*:

> At [this family's] previous church, the pastor had told them not to come back. . . . On occasion, [their son with Down syndrome] was energetic/disruptive, sometimes non-compliant, and a runner. Because of lack of training or willingness to include him in children's ministry, mom and dad had no alternative but to bring him into worship service with them, during which [their son] was at times unruly, loud, disruptive. . . . It was then the pastor, in a less-than-Christ-like way, shooed [this family] out of the church.[2]

OUR CHILD'S DEVELOPMENTAL AND PHYSICAL AGES DON'T MATCH

Our children may look like teens but still act like preschoolers. Or they may look and talk like their chronological age but, when frustrated, melt into toddlerhood. This is hard for youth leaders to handle and frustrating for our kids as they increasingly sense they're not like their friends. It's also more than a little anxiety inducing for parents of typically developing preschool kids to see our not-same-aged children participating when they don't seem to be in the right place. As our kids grow older, how do we handle summer sleep-away camps and their sleeping arrangements? Issues like these can become overwhelming for us, the staff, and the other families, and if we can't come up with a workable solution the whole church embraces, it can cause families like ours to simply stop trying.

PULPIT THEOLOGY AND OUR EXPERIENCES DON'T MATCH

Counselor Lucille Zimmerman explains this challenge in her book *Renewed*: "Many times Christians are taught to avoid emotional pain by being told, in so many words, that our emotions can't be trusted; therefore, we shouldn't acknowledge them."[3] She shares that, in her experience counseling church-attending clients who are grieving, they feel guilty because "church sometimes facilitates a message of moving quickly through pain by handing over Scripture and platitudes instead of encouraging the wrestling match . . . with the situation or with God."[4] As parents of children whose diagnoses color, challenge, and upend our lives regularly, we're not just periodically experiencing grief but living it daily. If a church preaches a "negative feelings are wrong" or a "swift grief" gospel, we feel left out and even judged for our struggles.

Even in the absence of a grief-averse culture, we can feel left out in our churches because instead of grace we find judgment. One mom and pastor's wife shared: "I think this causes the most stress for us because we would have expected (of all people) for those in our church family to be the most understanding and forgiving of our issues. And yet, at the moment we are finding that not to be the case." We're taught to forgive, to give grace, to turn the other cheek, and to love the unlovable, but in reality the message can feel like and be directly conveyed that there's a limit. And the threshold often can be lower than what our special families need.

The threshold of other people's
forgiveness, grace, longsuffering,
and love is often lower than what
our special families need.

WE FEEL SCRUTINIZED OR JUDGED

"It seems to me that we as mothers tend to always be looking around to see who is watching. I wish we could just support each other," commented Heather on Gillian Marchenko's blog post.[5] Anyone else notice this? I know I have, from just about my first moment as a mom. In the first months of raising our older two girls, I was the classic nervous first-time parent. Well-stocked diaper bag, consistent routine and nap times, conscientious of the surroundings, solicitous about my kids' needs, teaching them appropriate behavior, not feeding them too much sugar, no fast food—the whole shebang. Imagine my surprise when, the first time I took the girls to the park, I had to answer a two-minute business call on my old-school flip phone, and I had another mom comment loudly enough for me to hear, "Geesh, it's like she expects everyone else to watch her kids." Well, I *was* watching my kids.

Motherhood isn't for the faint of heart, that's for sure. Whether raising typically developing kids or higher needs kids, it can be a real judgment game. Maybe that's because parenting magazines so often portray families in color-coordinated outfits, with the mom/model made up, hair immaculate, and revealing no wrinkles, fatigue, stress, or other evidences of actual motherhood whatsoever. Maybe it's because we've read about that superwoman in Proverbs 31 who trades, sews, cooks, manages servants, loves her kids and husband, and gets up while it's still night to get started on it all for the next day. Or maybe it's because we're a bunch of fallen humans whose default posture is fear and insecurity. Probably a bit of all three. Whatever the reason, it isn't just us parents of special kids who face judgment and scrutiny.

But we may get a little extra dose of judgment because of our child's extra issues. The mom at the park I mentioned? She'd seen the kind of behavioral and sensory issues my kids had and could tell they were a handful. She didn't know that call was our escrow company with closing instructions for that day, or that it was important that I take it whether or not my kids were intense. All she seemed to resonate was that I wasn't doing my job well. My kids didn't suddenly get peaceful when my phone rang. They didn't get worse, but they remained loud and rowdy and needed me to keep an eye on them. The fact that I was doing that while talking wasn't good enough—and she made sure to let me know.

Maybe you've had that kind of interaction. The one where the look, comment, or actions of someone at church, in a store, or at a friend's home has made it clear you're not doing it right, at least in his or her opinion. Maybe, as one mom shared through my survey, you've faced a situation where "many people assume it's bad parenting when a child has behavior issues especially when a child doesn't 'look' like he has special needs." That scrutiny, that implicit judgment, is unmistakable. And it hurts deeply when we're trying to both raise our kids and continue living a functional life in the community.

WE FEEL DISCONNECTED FROM OTHER PARENTS RAISING KIDS THE SAME AGE

A dear friend of mine shared her experience with others with typically developing babies, confiding, "I feel like people don't understand. Like they thought I was making [my child's challenges] up or being dramatic or emotional. Friends would say things like, 'Wouldn't you feel better if we all went out to lunch together?' It was like they were from a different universe."

This is a struggle many of us share, and it leads to some of our most profound hurts as parents of special needs kids. The mom of a child with ADHD, sensory processing disorder, and epilepsy had this to say on the issue: "Most of our friends are no longer friends due to not being able to handle the issues that the kids have." She continued, "It is difficult because it leaves us feeling isolated and even though we love our kids, it leaves you wish[ing] just for one day that you had normal kids and that they could live a normal life."

Why does this happen? In part, we do it to ourselves. We listen to our friends talk about their kids and the fact that little Caitlin, four years younger than our child who looks "normal" on the outside, is doing something we're pretty sure our daughter won't be able to do . . . ever. A lot of the time we can manage the mental gymnastics required by these interactions through an internal dialogue that sounds something like this:

"My kids are different."
"It's okay that my kids are different."
"I can be happy about the accomplishments and milestones of my friend's child."
"I can appreciate my own child's milestones, even if nobody else notices them."

When we can't manage the internal dialogue, we hear ourselves thinking something else, something we'd never admit to anyone: "Why the heck can't my kid just do *one* thing like her age-peers?"

If we aren't distancing ourselves, sometimes our friends are beating a retreat. There are lots of reasons for this: the situation feels uncomfortable, they don't know what to say or how to help, or they feel guilty for having "normal" children when we're struggling with our "special" ones. Sometimes, as with our extended families, others assume our struggles aren't as hard as we make it out to be or that our kids shouldn't need such prolonged intervention or behavioral help, and we reach an impasse. One mom reports, "Some [friends] have flat out told me they don't believe the specialists' diagnosis. It's come to the point that I rarely discuss M's therapy with them or give updates." When that kind of disagreement happens, unless both parties put in the effort, the friendship fades.

WE WANT HELP BUT DON'T KNOW HOW TO ASK (OR WE GET UNHELPFUL HELP AND STOP ASKING ALTOGETHER)

While it's a huge gift to have meals or play groups arranged through church during the first challenging months after our special children's births or diagnoses, these simply aren't enough. We're still living the high-needs challenges every day, still facing new stressors as aspects of our children's conditions unfold and change over time. We feel bad about being needy for as long as we are. After all, from self-help books to church pulpits we're encouraged to pray more, buck up, and get on with it in faith!

But we can't. We can't get involved in church as much as we would like or feel we should. We may never be able to shop with our kids in tow. We may *still* struggle to get in a shower every day, just as we did as moms of newborns or newly-adopted. But it's been ten years, and that's weird— definitely not casserole-appropriate, right? So we start to pull back from church, play groups, and friendships. We judge ourselves as we think others are judging us (or maybe as some uncaring person actually *has* done) and shrink back from community.

Yet all the while we're hiding, we still need help. Some will continue to offer it, and we love them for it. Some have good intentions, but as

Michael, the father of a son with Fanconi anemia, shares, "Everyone always wants to know how they can help, but when you finally get beyond the pride and ask, sometimes that help is hard to come by." If they offer and follow through with help, they don't necessarily provide the help we wanted. They may bring a casserole when we really needed help picking up a prescription or a package at the post office. We need more than casseroles, so we get upset. What if part of our grieving process was accepting that other people can't read our minds and have their own issues on their plates (no pun intended)? The casserole's actually pretty great after all.

What if part of our grieving process
was accepting that other people
can't read our minds and have their
own issues on their plates?

And if our freezers are already chock-full of casserole love, perhaps as we forgive life for our situations being so hard we can do one of two things to give others in our communities the best possible shot at helping us when they can: designate someone to manage our lists of needs and act as the point person for people who want to help. Or send willing friends the link for *Special Families ... A Casserole's Not Enough*, which offers a whole section of practical ways to help, such as offering opportunities for respite, handyman services, or rides to clinic visits.[6]

WE WANT COMPASSION AND RELATIONSHIPS BUT GET STARES OR PITY

One mom, Lisa, addresses this issue as she confides, "My friends with neurotypical children have distanced themselves from me at times. I have felt their pity at times when I wished for their support." Another mom reflected, "No one really takes the time to find out what my life is really like. I hear a lot of 'I don't know how you do it' or 'you are amazing' but no one is truly there to listen and support." Oh, do I ever get that!

Yes, our families have ongoing needs. Yes, we've asked for prayer—a lot. Yes, we're in a continuously intense parenting role. And yet we wish we could walk into a room full of friends and have them ask about something other than how life is going with our special kids. It's awkward to be the ones people look at as though they feel sorry for us. It can feel as though we've been downgraded from friend status to charity case, a shift that imposes distance between people and carves out for us a role in relationships we haven't asked for: that of a martyr.

Even if the attitude doesn't dictate that role for us, it fashions a similar one: we are seen exclusively as special-needs parents. Which hurts us twice over since it reduces, stereotypes, and trivializes our identities and those of our children. Beth explained the challenge like this: "When I see them look at Lauren, I know they are seeing Down syndrome, not an actual living, breathing, deserving person. I usually avoid talking to people and going out, because I cannot stand seeing those looks. Also, I'm afraid I might hit someone, especially if they make a rude comment." We want the world to see our *kids*, not their diagnoses. We want the world to know us for *us*—for our strengths, quirks, spiritual gifts, personalities, and interests—not only in the context of one (albeit important) role as parents.

We want the world to know us for
us—for our strengths, quirks, spiritual
gifts, personalities, and interests—
not only in the context of one (albeit
important) role as parents.

When we feel ourselves diminished by this perception in community, we want to retreat and give up. Isolation seems so much easier, so much less frustrating. But it isn't real. As author and counselor Lucille Zimmerman notes in *Renewed*, "In Genesis 3, God said everything was good—and only called one thing not good: for man to be alone."[7] *Alone* isn't the answer, friend. Joy comes when we reframe our community experiences and pursue special versions of them that meet the deep needs of our hearts again.

PRACTICING FORGIVING OUR CHURCH AND COMMUNITY

- A day in the life. Spend a moment considering the perspectives of your friends or community members. Envision yourself in their lives, with their children, their challenges, their spouses, their financial issues, their childhood upbringings, their pain. Put them in a room with you. What feelings might they be feeling? What ways might they want to help, but not know what to say or how to ask? How do they feel about your struggle, your stress—about watching their friend or fellow churchgoer hurt for so long? From that perspective, allow yourself to release them—release you—from the words or actions that have hurt.
- You be the judge (or not). Consider or write down some times you've judged their parenting or their children's (mis)behavior. We've all done it, so let's just get honest here. Ask God's forgiveness for those moments, and for His help to extend the grace you long for to others when they make the same mistakes we have.

Thirteen

REBUILDING JOY IN COMMUNITY

"The best moments—and most agonizing ones—
occur at the intersection of two people."
—Tom Rath and Jim Harter, *Wellbeing*

Eleanor Roosevelt said a lot of memorable things, but one quote attributed to her could be our mantra as we face and attempt to engage effectively with church, friendships, and community: "Do one thing every day that scares you." We get hurt by people and scared to assert ourselves, but in order for us to experience joy we have to bind up those wounds and take the risk of engaging yet again. If not for our happiness, at least for our physical health. Bestselling author Tom Rath, who focuses on living our strengths, has this to say: "There is something about having close friendships in general that is good for our physiological health. Relationships serve as a buffer during tough times, which in turn improves our cardiovascular functioning and decreases stress levels."[1] Once we've begun the work of forgiving and letting go of hurts in friendship and community, here are a few ideas of ways to actively work toward joy in our relationships.

BE PRESENT IN THE MOMENT

It's hard enough today to invest in our friendships and faith communities without letting old hurts weigh us down. Once we've done the work of forgiving perceived and intentional slights (and commit to continue doing so!), we have to grab on to something else or we'll slide back into the pity party or isolation. What better thing to grab on to than right now? This moment . . . the present.

Some circles refer to this as "being mindful" or "practicing mindfulness." The term may seem new-age-y or navel-gaze-ish at first, but don't let it fool you. In essence, it means to be aware—to focus our thoughts on the present moment, as opposed to our shopping lists, kids' challenges, schedules, or anything else.[2] (Is anyone else already feeling more peaceful just thinking about not thinking about all that?) Once we let ourselves temporarily set aside external pressures and looming needs, mindfulness lets us notice our feelings, thoughts, physical sensations, and what's going on around us . . . in this moment.

What does this have to do with friendships or community? Dr. Mark Myers, department chair for the Center for Counseling and Family Studies at Liberty University, offers a clue: "There is something about being present in a non-judgmental or non-reactive way that enhances the regulatory processes of emotion."[3] In other words, when we know how to be mindful—aware, in the moment—we're less apt to live in the whirlwinds of emotion and grief that may have colored our pasts. Instead, we're right here, right now. And even if it's hard right here, right now, it's just this one moment we're dealing with, instead of dragging along its 101 closest cousins as well.

It's this mindfulness concept to which I believe Jesus was referring when He encouraged "do not be anxious about your life . . . Look at the birds of the air: they neither sow nor reap nor gather into barns, and yet your heavenly Father feeds them. Are you not of more value than they? And which of you by being anxious can add a single hour to his span of life?" (Matthew 6:25–27 ESV). Jesus—human skin of God who's outside time—tells us in this passage, I believe, a part of what it is to have the mind of Christ: Be all *here*. Look to God *in this moment*—in regard to community relationships or any other aspect of life. Let the rest go.

Be all *here*. Look to God *in this
moment*—in regard to community
relationships or any other aspect of life.
Let the rest go.

We can't unmake the past or control the future. We can't add one hour to our lives, or change the people we know, or predict what they may do in the moments ahead. What we *can* do, however, is be all here, fully *with* the people we're with. We can maximize the potential God has built into us and expect His goodness and grace to be with us as we love people and walk through life in tandem. If our minds and feelings are anywhere other than in the present moment, if we're anything but mindful in our interactions with our friends or communities, we miss out on joy we'll never be able to recoup—the particular joy that is only available to us right now. I don't know about you, but I can't afford to pass up joy, even if it *is* wrapped in the complexity of relationship. Can you?

BE A COMPASSION AMBASSADOR

Counterintuitive as it may sound, this one comes a lot easier once we've had life beat us up a bit. The apostle Paul enthuses, "Blessed be the God and Father of our Lord Jesus Christ, the Father of mercies and God of all comfort, who comforts us in all our affliction, so that we may be able to comfort those who are in any affliction, with the comfort with which we ourselves are comforted by God" (2 Corinthians 1:3–4 ESV). Even on our hardest days we can recall ways in which God has comforted us, undergirded us, shorn us up, and shown us mercy. One of my favorite ways to get my joy back (and feel like a still-functional human) with friends and at church is to turn around and pass that comfort along. On days when everything stinks (encopresis is on one of my girls' diagnostic rosters, so we're talking actual and figurative stench here), to reach out is to truly live.

I love how blogger Megan Goates conveys what life as the mom of a child with special needs has done to her humility level. In a post she begins with a tantalizing "Ten years ago I was the perfect mom," she reveals how the ways in which she's been challenged have enhanced her relationships with friends and her community:

> We (meaning me) are way less smug. In fact, we (me) acknowledge that most of the time, we don't know what the heck we are doing. We have more patience with people. We have less patience for unnecessary activities, which deplete our time and energy. We've learned to sometimes say *no* when we are asked to do things because anything extra usually takes us past the tipping point. We care less about *stuff*. We are gentler. We feel genuine empathy for someone else's hardship. We aren't anywhere near perfect. We don't even care about perfect. We think perfect should be dropkicked down the street.[4]

I'm willing to bet most of us could tell similar stories of how our lives have changed us, broken us, humbled us, and, ultimately, equipped us with something that comes only with years and experience: true compassion. That attitude of seeing into the hearts and needs of others enough not only to empathize but to roll up our sleeves and walk the road with them—to bear one another's burdens, as we're exhorted to do in Galatians 6:2. It's this burden-bearing, compassionate quality that made the famous "good Samaritan" good (see Luke 10:33).

Compassion is also what led Jesus to heal people's diseases and feed thousands by means of miracles (Matthew 14:14 and 15:32). It's what led Him to comfort and minister to them, as He perceived that "they were harassed and helpless, like sheep without a shepherd" (Matthew 9:36). He'd relinquished all of His divine prerogatives, having left heaven to live in a limited, decaying human body that would ultimately be rejected and crucified by His own people (see Philippians 2:7; Isaiah 53:3). He experienced more loss and brokenness than any one of us will ever face, causing His compassion to swell and pour out for others every day.

We can offer others comfort and compassion too. No, they aren't going through the exact same situations, but we're all facing challenges, perhaps even feeling as though they're just about as hard as we can possibly bear in this very moment. Even as we recognize this in our own lives, we can ask God to soften our hearts toward friends and neighbors—to help us find ways to share the comfort He is continuously offering us in our own struggles. In doing that we open doors—and maybe even flood-gates—for joy.

ONCE YOU ASK FOR HELP . . . RECEIVE IT

Part of the reason it's hard for us to connect with and maintain friends is that we're barely muddling through ourselves, let alone having emotional or physical energy in reserve to reach out to friends or to our church. We've bought into the notion that in order to initiate or maintain a friendship we've got to have our acts together. Which makes asking for help just about impossible. As one mom, Kaci, admitted, "Some days I wake up and feel like I have an elephant on my chest just holding me in bed and making it hard to breathe. It took me a very long time to learn to ask for help."[5]

That's understandable. I've been there too—in that place where I'm so overwhelmed by the behavior modification, medical appointments, therapies, meal planning, and trying to find time to take a shower that it's more work to explain and equip others to help with our needs than it is to handle them ourselves. That's what we tell ourselves anyway. We can have joy in our community and friendships by loosening our vice grip on life enough to give others permission to love and connect with us. And we can do so in reliance on *their* strengths instead of allowing our anxiety to restrict their efforts.

Fellow church members or friends may not understand how we do things, why we do them, or the value of what we're doing, but they do love us. Let's allow them to love us in the ways they do it best. If they're good at making meals, let them know they can bring one by whenever they feel led. If they're good at organization, let them come over and help you get one season's clothes stored away and another's organized. If they love to clean, invite them over for breakfast and let them help you with the tasks you dread tackling in your house. Unleash their strengths as often as they offer. They'll feel good about helping in ways that optimize their interests, and you'll get over feeling like a helpless clod as you laugh and sip coffee together and get to know them and their struggles too.

Fellow church members or friends
may not understand how we do
things, why we do them, or the
value of what we're doing, but they
do love us. Let's allow them to love
us in the ways they do it best.

LEARN HOW TO SAY NO . . . AND WHEN TO SAY YES

Perhaps you can relate to emails and voice mails like these that I've
gotten:

> "Mrs. Wallin? Hi, this is Marion from the school. We need some
> things for the holiday party in class tomorrow. Will you bring
> [something that takes more hours than you've got in the day to
> prepare]?"

> "Hi Laurie, this is Andie. Someone stepped down from this task
> at church. Can you fill in for a few [years] months?"

> "Hey, honey. Can we [you] make that new [two-hour prep time]
> recipe for dinner tonight?"

"Parent" can sometimes seem synonymous with "vending machine."
Sometimes I love meeting needs and helping people around me. But if
I'm not careful—if I say yes to too much, or for the wrong reasons—my
"help" comes off more like anger, sarcasm, annoyance, frustration, or
resentment.

Been there? Scripture tells us that God (and everyone else!) loves a
"cheerful giver" (2 Corinthians 9:7). So how can we be that kind of community participant without it knocking the wind out of our sails? For
one thing, we can learn when it's appropriate to say yes and when it isn't.
From the many times I've agreed to do something when I should have

declined I can share a few ways to help you determine whether yes is the
right answer to a need that comes up:

It honors God in that it acts on your faith or fulfills a part of what you
feel you were created to do. Or, if the task isn't precisely in line with
your lifelong calling, perhaps that yes makes sense based on what you
feel God is calling you to do *for this season.* (Which doesn't mean trying
to be perfect or save the world.) Perhaps that yes stretches your faith a
little too. The assignment may be out of your comfort zone, but it's in
line with what you believe—in *whom* you believe—and feels as though
it's worth the risk.

It honors your strengths and talents. The task or decision fits in with
what you're good at. It gives you energy rather than sapping it. Or maybe
it opens the door to a dream that's been brewing in your heart. That *yes*
may be the first step of faith toward doing something you've longed to do
for a while. Accepting and following through takes guts, but the prospect
energizes you at the same time, just as using your strengths does.

It builds relationship. It deepens and supports a friendship or family
bond because it's life-affirming to others. Perhaps it helps, comforts, supports, or refuels others or provides opportunity for conversation and
connection. Maybe that yes represents a first step toward redeeming a
loss or mending a rift in a relationship—whether caused by you or someone else—and can begin to rebuild burned bridges.

And, of course, we know when a yes is right because it brings us joy.
Not happiness, which hinges on circumstances, but joy that's heart-deep,
unshakable, and independent of what anyone else may think of our yes
or no. Whatever the reason, when we're intentional and give within the
context of our larger vision for life and people, we can say yes whole-
heartedly and enjoy the ride! If a need that comes doesn't fit one of these
criteria, maybe it's time to respond with the hardest word ever: *no.* (With
a warm smile, of course.) That two-letter word? It can be almost painful
to utter for us parents whose family needs make it hard to feel like the

productive, generous members of the community we wish we could be. But it's a crucial addition to our working vocabularies. Being able to say no, even if we feel obliged to do so frequently, means that we're implicitly saying a bigger yes—to God's best for us or others. And that's a reason for joy.

BE THE FRIEND YOU WANT THEM TO BE

> Whatever you wish that others would do to you, do also to them, for this is the Law and the Prophets. (Matthew 7:12 ESV)

My husband jokes that we need a military-grade logistics team to plan date nights or midday get-togethers with a friend! That isn't far from the truth. As we've discussed, one of the hardest aspects of raising kids with special needs can be the isolation. It's just really hard to maintain close friendships when life is dictated by all the appointments our kids need in order to thrive, let alone survive, in their unique situations.

We don't have all the time in the
world, but we can still be good
friends—the kind of friends we
want to have—to the people close
to our hearts.

We don't have all the time in the world, but we can still be good friends—the kind of friends we want to have—to the people close to our hearts. Following is a list of ways we can do that, even from inside the mess of scheduling, treatments, and tantrums that defines and constrains our lives:

Be willing to make the first move. Call them first, even if it's been a few weeks (months). Send notes, cards, or gifts. I signed up for a $10/month service called Send Out Cards because it's an easy way to send cards and gifts. Since the points I buy expire, the "I don't want to waste money" mind-set motivates me to use them to connect with the people I love.

Be interested in their lives. Listen when they talk without trying to formulate in your mind what you'll say next. Ask them about their lives and about whatever you talked about together the last time. Encourage them in their dreams. Celebrate their milestones and successes. Remember their big days. Honor their choices. Pray for them. Get excited about what their kids accomplish. Offer them a piece of your chocolate. Tell them when they have something in their teeth. (Those are the real friends, right?)

Be honest and open with them. Don't sugarcoat your life when they ask about it, but don't let your stories dominate the conversation either. Have a sense of humor and mirror what they find funny (which may not be gallows humor about hemophilia treatments or giant sensory meltdowns in McDonald's). Tell them how much they mean to you, even if it feels weird to throw that in at the end of a conversation.

Be there. I know this seems like a no-go with everything we're balancing in our families, but bear with me. Dependability means that whatever you're able to do, you do as consistently as you can. Be loyal. Keep a confidence. Call when you say you will (or let them know why you can't). Be as accessible as you can. Answer texts from those closest to you (or who you want to be better friends with) in a timely manner. It takes ten seconds to send a sentence back to a friend on our phones. We've got ten seconds, people.

This may seem to be a tall order, and I'm sure you could add even more to these categories! I screw up just about every one of them over the course of any given month, but the people who let me keep trying are the ones worth trying for. Some I see and talk to every week. Others live far away, and their friendship resides primarily in my heart at this point. But I'm so grateful for the ways they each reveal the love of God in their love for me. Chances are you've got a friend or two—maybe more—who respond to your efforts and love you through the ups and downs. The joy exuding from friendships with these individuals can motivate us to invest energy with them as much as we can, which fuels even more joy!

REMEMBER THE UNEXPECTED GOOD IN COMMUNITY

It's happened to us—so many times I can't begin to count. The time my college roommate's mom called out of the blue to offer to bring us a meal. Nothing new was happening in our family. She was just thinking of us and wanted to love us with food. Or the time a toilet failed in our house and when I texted my good friend to whine about it, her husband showed up on our doorstep to take me to Home Depot, pick out a new toilet, and install it himself. This couple has known us and our kids' needs long enough to understand the stress that something as "simple" as needing to replace a toilet can mean in terms of logistics and finances. But *knowing* about and *doing something* about a situation are the difference between being acquainted with someone and being loved by them like crazy. My former roommate's mom, as well as my other friend and her husband, have many times embodied love in action, unexpectedly. And they're by no means the only ones.

Kathryn Sneed, a fellow writer at SpecialNeedsParenting.net, shares a story in one of her posts about a complete stranger showing this kind of love for her family. She'd been in a Chick-fil-A with her then-toddler son who's been diagnosed with autism and sensory processing disorder. She writes,

> We parked, walked in, and ordered. Everything was going great until we sat down and I set up the food. That was when the meltdown started. Screaming, kicking, crying. I hadn't even had a bite of my food yet! Everyone was looking at us, so I took him out of the high chair and went into the ladies' room to help calm him down for a few minutes. We talked, he finished crying and calmed down a bit, and we walked back out. I put him back in the high chair and sat down to eat.
>
> Only two minutes later it started again, only this time worse. Crying, screaming, kicking and more . . . I decided it was time to

leave, but I couldn't even leave my son to pack up our food. By this time he had almost tipped over his high chair so I took him out. He laid on the floor continuing his meltdown. Then out of nowhere this lady with a kind smile came behind me and packed all our food up. She made it so nothing would spill and handed it over to me. . . . It was such a small thing, but it made my day and was something that I hope to never forget.[6]

That last sentence? That's another key to joy in community: intentionally remembering the good. It can be tough to do since in moments like the one Kathryn describes we're so pumped full of adrenaline as we rush to exit the scene of craziness that we can barely see straight, let alone thoughtfully consider details of what's happening. And there's that tendency we've talked about—the way our brains more strongly recall negative emotions and memories than positive ones. It takes deliberate effort to note the good gifts in community. But joy lives in the moments in which we make that choice. That choice to be grateful for whatever it is that's good and right in our interactions with people we know, and even with total strangers who love us when we need it most.

Fourteen

IS GOD EVEN LISTENING?
("FORGIVING" GOD)

*"I feel at times that God has abandon[ed] me. He left me in the wilderness
and when I cry out for Him to heal my daughter, I get silence."*
—Ashley, mom of a child with Mowat-Wilson syndrome

Forgiving God. That's quite a topic. Theologically, of course, we can't
forgive God; forgiveness is for those who've done something wrong. If
we trust Scripture as truth, we understand that God is completely righteous—the very definition and embodiment of right-ness—and that
"there is no wickedness in him" (Psalm 92:15).

Theologically, we can't forgive God. But emotionally—well, that's a
different story. As with the biblical Job, at some point in our lives as
parents God found His way into the crosshairs of our anger, resentment,
depression, and stress. His thoughts and ways may be higher than ours,
and His wisdom beyond finding out (Isaiah 55:9; Romans 11:33), but that
hasn't kept us from trying, from probing and prodding and pressing Him
for answers to the questions that weigh heavily on us every time we look
at our children as they struggle to walk, breathe, trust, focus, relate . . .
survive. We can't technically forgive God, but we must *do something with*
Him, with His sovereignty, with His hand in all of this. If we don't, there's
always going to be that elephant in the room—the feeling we hold in, the
same feeling Job describes at the end of his story: "I cry to you, O God, but

you don't answer. I stand before you, but you don't even look. You have become cruel toward me. You use your power to persecute me. You throw me into the whirlwind and destroy me in the storm" (Job 30:20–22 NLT).

We can't technically forgive God, but if we don't do *something* with Him, none of the work we've done so far in this book or in our lives as parents matters. Like Peter we find ourselves, after all our grieving and striving, facing Jesus's perennial question "Who do you say that I am?" (Mark 8:29 ESV). As much as we put it off, feel guilty about it, and try to overcompensate with spiritual practices and service, we circle back around to this one question, to the reality that the meaning we fight so hard to find in our situation hinges on this one relationship.

Why is this topic last if it's so important? Because, as one mom confided, "For a couple of years after [my child's] diagnosis, I was angry with God, but it took me awhile to realize that."

As in a couple of years, friends.

Years.

For those of us who consider ourselves Christians, we face a few big questions:

"If God is able to heal my child, why doesn't He?"

"Is God not healing my child (or this situation) because of something I did?"

"If this is because of something I did, why won't God tell me what I need to change?"

"If God is in control of everything, what's the difference between His *allowing* my child's challenges and His *causing* them?"

These questions can agitate just beneath the surface for a long time before we allow ourselves to acknowledge them. If the process doesn't take years, then perhaps it will take a couple of other "somethings" to bring them to the fore, to push us to the audacity of formulating the thoughts. Like maybe a couple of new stressors thrown into the mix— for us it was when my husband lost his job just as our younger adopted daughter's decline forced us to admit her to a residential psychiatric treatment facility. Or perhaps it will take a couple of new diagnoses. As one mom revealed, "I was upset about [my child's] condition but I don't think I blamed anyone. I just thought, it is what it is. However when [my younger child] had a heart defect, I was mad at God."

That first challenge we can muscle through. It may dent our faith—maybe even come close to bashing it in—but history and adrenaline carry us through. The second one, though? Jackie, the mom of two, shared, "When my daughter developed an autoimmune disorder at six years old, I really struggled. She went to bed fine and woke up completely different the next day. Why would God take a part of both of my kids? Why would a loving God let children suffer?"

For our family the question extends back in retrospect to the earlier years in foster care God allowed our older girls to endure before they became ours—years that shredded their ability to attach to the people who love them, on top of the mental health and developmental disabilities they each have.

WHY WOULD GOD ALLOW OUR CHILDREN— OR US—TO SUFFER?

I'm not a theologian, but here's what I know: "In this world you will have trouble," says Jesus. "But take heart! I have overcome the world" (John 16:33). And I can vouch from experience that this is true . . . *both* parts. When Jesus says "overcome" in that verse, He isn't talking about negating the first part of the "promise" (as we wish He would). There's still trouble afoot, and it still trips us up. We all find ourselves regularly in the apostle Peter's place on the stormy waters. As with Peter, a storm rears up in our lives—maybe at the first diagnosis, or maybe long before that when we first suspect something isn't right. At some point after the onset of the first squall, we muster enough faith to address God: "Father, if you are willing, take this cup from me; yet not my will, but yours be done" (Luke 22:42). Even if we manifest only three seconds' worth of faith, it draws us, like Peter, out of the boat—moving way beyond what we thought we knew about storms into the roaring surge. In that moment we lock eyes with our Lord long enough to realize that getting through the tempest will entail pressing as close to Jesus as possible—even if that means walking *on* the raging sea of the unknown.

At some point we're hefted back into the boat with Jesus, the storm dies down, and life goes on for a day, a month . . . maybe even a few years. But another storm invariably arises—when we get discouraged after a visit to the specialist; those test results come back more alarming than we had hoped; we feel the weariness of nonstop asking, seeking, and knocking in prayer for our kids (Luke 11:9)—and we turn accusing eyes toward Jesus, challenging Him, as Job did: "You, [God], have become cruel toward me. . . . You throw me into the whirlwind." If we would only gaze at Him for longer than a second, not as the God who would/could change our circumstances, but as the God who grieves—who wept over His child too—just maybe we'd hear it: "The storm has been going since Adam and Eve's sinful choice, my child, and I've been steadying you on the waves ever since."

HOW TO DEAL WITH GOD AND OUR GRIEF

In her book *Forgiving God: A Woman's Struggle to Understand When God Answers No*, Carla McClafferty recounts how she spent the first months after her toddler son died of accidental injury: alternating between ignoring God, feeling numb, and shooting God dirty looks from across her heart. Day after day she faced the reality of life as a stay-at-home mom—a life that had once seemed not to have enough hours in a day—wishing each new day would end the moment she awoke in the morning. The reality of her family's new normal loomed large in her heart and weighed heavily on her soul. Life would never again be the way it was. She would never again wrap her arms around her little boy. Her older son wouldn't talk about it, her preschool daughter cried inconsolably, and Carla went through the motions from a "hole of misery so deep my screams of grief were without sound. A place so sad, my tears ran dry. A place so empty, I could not pray. A place so bitter, I didn't want to pray."[1]

Been there? I know I have. Even though my children live, grief has brought me to that place time and time again—once in the car after taking the older two girls to a court-appointed visit with their birth mom. She'd greeted and hugged the older one, but when the younger reached chubby hands in the air and squealed "Mommy!" she was too engrossed in the older child to notice. I saw a little of that beautiful toddler's light die in that moment. Her eyes took on a distant glaze as her arms slowly sank to her lap. She didn't call out again, didn't look to me for help. Just sat, empty. I screamed at God then. Screamed and banged fists on the steering wheel later that day while the girls were with my mom. Screamed and wept hot salt tears—tears welling up from a grief so deep, so sad, so bitter I wondered if God even noticed, since He clearly wasn't seeing my future daughter's grief or protecting this tiny girl from such pain.

I've been there more recently too. At the pizza parlor, holding my third daughter after she'd toddled some of her first steps, grabbed a chair for support, and ended up falling backward onto the hard floor, the chair on top of her. She had what looked like a seizure then; her eyes rolled back and she went limp. I breathed for her until she started breathing on her own again. For the next year and a half she experienced unexplained seizures that didn't follow any pattern neurologists could identify, every few weeks collapsing in a seizure and then going unconscious for sixty or more seconds. I held her in my arms time after time, begging her to wake up. I held her in doctors' offices time after time, begging them to help her not have to go through this. I held it together in our family as best I could, with our two just-adopted preschoolers whose special needs were already more than enough to handle. I'd close myself in the bedroom closet and scream and weep. I wasn't sure whether God heard or, if He did, whether He'd do anything about the situation. I'd already experienced His silence—His implicit no—time and again on behalf of my older two.

And then there was the most recent incident. Still fresh, still in many ways raw for me. I'll share it through an excerpt from my book *Why Your Weirdness Is Wonderful*:

> The younger of [our adopted girls] arrived with the diagnosis "failure to thrive"; it doesn't take a medical degree to get the gist of what that means. Over the next two years, we helped her reach a normal weight and growth rate for a preschooler, but then things started going downhill—this time, mentally and emotionally instead of physically.
>
> With each new troubling behavior or symptom, my "make a difference" quirk led me to do whatever I could to help her. We

embarked on years of weekly behavioral therapy, and hundreds of hours in multiple hospital departments to discover what was keeping her inner growth stunted and her mood swings and toilet behaviors unresponsive to treatment. After five years of uphill battle for my little girl, it became clear we couldn't manage her the way she needed. We admitted her to a psychiatric hospital on our doctor's recommendation.

At that point, my "make a difference" trait was pretty bruised up, worn out, and discouraged. As with any deep-seated tendency, though, it drove me. I tried and tried and tried with our girl—trying to make a difference, trying to live my strengths and quirks wonderfully—but I felt like more and more of a failure.

On the day she was due to be discharged from the hospital and return home, I sat in a tiny fluorescent-lit room, listening to the social worker. Her voice overly soothing, she listed all the time-intensive follow-up appointments my daughter would need (on top of what was already in place), and a quiet word formed on my lips: "No." The social worker's shocked look mirrored my feelings, but I said it again anyway: "No. My daughter cannot come home."[2]

That day I packed up my not-so-little-anymore girl—the one who'd been snubbed by her birth mom—and drove her not home but to a large complex where she would live for God only knew how long. And I wondered, as I willed myself to drive away, tears streaking lines down my cheeks, "*Does* God know? Does He see? I mean, if He did, why the hell are we in this situation with a little girl He could have advocated for years ago?!"

IT'S TIME TO GET ANGRY

Thus began my angry phase. "Hell" was the first of a long, sordid string of words this Christian woman uttered to—no, *spat at*—God. I swore, screamed, and wept. I'd yell and rant at Him until I couldn't think of anything else to say, then feel so instantly guilty that I'd feel compelled to numb the pain. I was so emotionally exhausted that I let myself give up on working out. I couldn't make the angry/guilty feelings stop, so I began to drink a glass of wine each evening—sometimes two. Or three—to quiet the noise inside. I'd watch reruns on Netflix until my mind relented and allowed me to fall asleep. Whatever it took to escape the anger and make my mind and its grief leave me alone.

When I wasn't escaping and found myself accidentally present with my thoughts, I'd again turn the full fury of my grief toward the only One who *could* do anything about any of this . . . but hadn't. What kind of God allows sisters—one thirteen months old, the other just two months—to bounce through *seven* placements before the failed adoption that landed them in my life? He'd known what that would do to their minds, to their ability to function and attach to the human race. What kind of messed up God would turn a blind eye to that degree of injustice, of evil? What kind of God would allow my second daughter's struggles to be impervious to all interventions, to the point that the one doctor we trust and appreciate more than any other throws his hands in the air, admitting "I've never felt so helpless with a patient"? This, after my having endured countless other specialists and therapists who treated me as though I were making it all up, as I clawed my way through the health-care system trying to find help for my daughter who'd never really stopped failing to thrive. What kind of God would drag out a child's healing, ignore her need, watch her struggle and do . . . nothing?

Have you finally come to the end
of trying hard? Have you allowed
yourself to fully face God and get
real about your struggle?

There was more, of course, but I don't need to delineate it all here, because you could fill in the rest. That is, if you've finally come to the end of trying hard and have allowed yourself to turn, to fully face God and get real about your struggle. If you haven't, may I suggest that it's time? Might you be willing to consider taking Carla McClafferty's example, below, and making it your own prayer of spitting rage?

The house was silent when I returned [from the first time drop-ping off just one child at childcare at church after my son died]. I felt I could not live one more hour. . . . For the first time . . . I fell to my knees and poured out my rage to God. I told him how I honestly felt. I cried and screamed my way through every bitter thought and emotion, regardless of how blasphemous it was. I honestly told God the feelings I had. When I was through vent-ing my rage, I asked God to give me peace in my heart to make it through the next hour.[3]

WE CAN'T "FORGIVE" GOD UNTIL WE FACE HIM

We can't face a God we're not sure is listening, in control, or good, without taking it in bite-sized pieces. In her book McClafferty goes on to slowly unfold what it is to face God, yell at Him, tire, regroup, face God, yell at Him, tire, and regroup until the anger fizzles out in exhaustion and we're ready to consider relating again. This isn't a one-time interac-tion. For us, most of whose children still live, our grief continues to cycle with new symptoms and diagnoses, so we'll go through this rage with God to varying degrees over and over again. Which is another reason for us to get good at letting ourselves get good and angry. If we're trying to hold it in, the chances are we'll still be holding one stunted grieving pro-cess in our hearts when the next one hits. Who needs that kind of crazy?

Ironically, it's in this one-moment-at-a-time releasing of rage that we become open to authentic relationship with God. As someone once said, you don't know what people are really like until you fight with them. It's only when we let ourselves fight and argue with God—when we wrap our arms tightly around Him in a chokehold and demand a response, as Jacob did so long ago (see Genesis 32)—that we find our-selves close enough to hear Him. To hear the voice that is at once the rush of many waters and the softest of whispers in our darkest moments. To feel His universe-releasing, courage-imbuing breath on our cheeks. To see in His eyes the tears that linger from His own sac-rificial grief of that day when His Son, maimed by humanity, squeezed Himself into the brokenness of flesh and then died so we could live to wrestle with God at all.

It's this exhausting wrestling, moment by moment and day by day, that places us close enough that, when we're spent and collapse into depression, we fall into the only arms that can really console us in our grief and loss.

THE REALITY OF "FORGIVING" GOD

It may be a theological impossibility to forgive God—it may seem blasphemous to even mention the idea—but whatever we call it the transaction has to happen if we're to get back our joy in this life as parents. When we're finally over being angry, when we've fallen into the arms of the One we may still not be sure we can trust completely, we must take one step more. We have to let Him reveal Himself to us. We have to be willing to give Him the chance to reveal His love for us again. I'm not actually talking about something *we* do or muster or pursue. *It's all Him.* God is where the buck finally stops. God is the One who could have made our lives anything else, but for His own inscrutable reasons chose to make them the way they are. God is all-powerful—most of us will concede that. But after we survive our rage at Him, we need to open our eyes to see the flip side, to experience what it means that *God is love* (1 John 4:8). It's quite possible for many of us that this may entail seeing it *again.* For others of you reading this it may be a first glimpse. Either way, allow me to reiterate that God doesn't expect us to come to Him. No, God takes the initiative in coming to us. He has *always* come to us (John 3:16).

God doesn't expect us to come to Him.
No, God takes the initiative in coming
to us. He has always come to us.

We can begin to entertain this strange idea of forgiving God when we challenge Him like this (go ahead; He's okay with it): "You allowed me to hurt. You allowed my child to hurt. You could stop (or could have stopped) it but You don't, and I don't understand. But I want to see You, to see goodness in my life again. I want to be reconciled with You. I want

to know I'm not alone in this. I need You to show me who You are."
You and I are by no means the first to do this. Moses, when the people God had asked him to lead out of captivity kept figuratively running
back toward it, challenged God like this: "Show me your glory" (Exodus
33:18). That word *glory*, in the original Hebrew, is *kabowd*, which refers
to "the weight of something, but only figuratively in a good sense."[4]
Christian speaker and author John Bevere explains it further: "Its definition also speaks of splendor, abundance, and honor. Moses was asking,
'Show me Yourself in all Your splendor.'"[5]

Moses's example opens the door for us to reconcile with God when
we've been hurt, and especially when we feel it's *He* who's hurt us the
most: ask God to show you the weight, the essence, of who He is. Because
grief distorts our knowledge of God. It can seem to snuff out what little
trust we had in Him. The only way to open that door, to move through
grief and toward healing in our relationship with God, is to ask Him to
remind us who He really is.

Are we going to want to be intimate with Him all the time? No. Are
we still going to feel rage swelling up toward God as new grief comes our
way? Of course. But I hope you'll allow me, as a fellow parent walking
this imperfect road of life with special kids, to share my experience: this
is the only way to truly, deeply, and in lasting ways get your joy back.

PRACTICING "FORGIVING" GOD

- Be honest. Say what you're feeling, even if the way you express it
  would humiliate you if someone were to repeat it to your friends
  and family. Let God have it—the good, the bad, and the ugly.
  Because it's only in honesty, in letting ourselves get mad, that we
  let God close enough to help us begin to heal.
- Open your eyes. Ask God, as Moses did, to show you His glory.
  Then sit tight while He does. You may be mad—even while you're
  asking. (I often am. I get that!) But that's okay. It's real, and it's a
  step in the right direction. The direction from which joy and healing can find you again.

Fifteen

REDISCOVERING JOY WITH GOD

"Wrestling with God in the midst of painful emotions such as anger and grief becomes the arena in which we can finally understand that life is hard but God is good."
—Lucille Zimmerman, *Renewed*

The idea of joy occurs over two hundred times in the Bible—more times than "forgiveness," "salvation," or "grace."[1] This sets the Christian faith apart from other worldviews, because "the joy of the LORD is your strength" (Nehemiah 8:10). Contrary to secular humanism or eastern traditions, joy isn't a state of mind we need to earn.[2] It's a gift God gives; as Charles Spurgeon once pointed out, "We are not left to search for joy; it is brought to our doors by the love of God our Father; joy refined and satisfying, befitting immortal spirits."[3] I don't know about you, but just knowing that joy is hand-delivered by God to my door is overwhelmingly wonderful to this weary, too-many-doctor-appointments-and-IEP-meetings mama!

If we don't have to earn or conjure it, how *do* we rediscover this joy of the Lord—our strength—in our hearts and families?

REMEMBER THE GIFTS

In her book *The Wall Around Your Heart*, Mary DeMuth offers one way to let God's joy back in. She writes, "If I've learned one thing on this earth, it's this: people who live in gratitude toward God have the most joyful lives."[4] People who *live in gratitude*. "Well," you may be thinking, "that leaves me out!" Or maybe not. Either way, living in gratitude is still a restorer of joy with God, and it's possible to do so without feeling happy first—whew!—by simply deciding to recognize and acknowledge what is good right now. Not pretending that something bad is good (that's denial) or making up good things that aren't actually happening (that's psychosis) but noticing the good in this moment.

Ann Voskamp, in her book *One Thousand Gifts*, shares, "Losses [tear holes in us]. One life-loss can infect the whole of a life. Like a rash that wears through our days, our sight becomes peppered with black voids. Now everywhere we look, we only see all that isn't."[5] Gratitude, which her book masterfully coaches readers to live, fills in the holes. It doesn't remove those holes—that would dishonor our pain and grief. It doesn't paint over or somehow camouflage them—that would just put grief on hold until it can't wait anymore. It fills the holes with something totally different, life-giving.

Even if we're tired, disappointed, or leaving a heart-breaking meeting at the school on behalf of our kids, we can be grateful for the sunshine, the shoes we're no doubt wearing, the air in our lungs, the fact that our kids have the chance to attend school, the homes we'll return to, the transportation we'll take there. Be careful, though. Once you start noticing the gifts in your life, it's hard to stay upset. It takes a lot of work to doubt God's goodness while considering a thousand good things He's provided and accomplished in your life!

Beyond the present moment, practicing gratitude invites joy and health in the future too. As Lucille Zimmerman expresses in her book *Renewed*, "Grateful people report fewer incidences of stress and depression compared to those who focus on neutral or negative aspects of their lives."[6] Gratitude not only grows your joy and happiness right now, but by releasing endorphins (happy hormones) in your body, its joy-ensuring value extends into the future.

STOP ASKING "WHY?" AND START ASKING "HOW?"

Nothing sucks away our joy with God more than those pesky *whys*. Questions like, Why did God allow this? Why is my child suffering despite the best interventions? Why doesn't God help that doctor listen to me? Why isn't God listening to me? Scripture so beautifully reminds us that "'my thoughts are nothing like your thoughts,' says the LORD. 'And my ways are far beyond anything you could imagine'" (Isaiah 55:8 NLT). We know this, but we're curious (and angry and needing to stop the madness), so we keep trying anyway. Just like Job. He held on through days, weeks, months—maybe longer?—in agony, grieving loss after loss. Then he let God have it. After a multi-chapter defense of his character, inferring that God had no reason to permit all the trouble to happen in his life, he concluded with, if you'll allow me to paraphrase, "Why won't God confront me and tell me His judgments like any other king so I can defend myself?" (see Job 31:35–36).

God responds with, in essence, "I'm sorry, but did I just hear you judging the infinite Being who gave you life and created this entire universe, down to the atomic particles that form it?" (see Job 38–40).

When we ask why, we miss the point. Whys implicitly accuse God, while hows invite Him to show up and work miracles.

When we ask why, we miss the point, as Job did at his weakest moment. *Whys* implicitly accuse God, while *hows* invite Him to show up and work miracles. They tug us outside ourselves, outside the box and into God's ballpark, where His goodness and wonder reign. The shift might look like this:

Not "Why did God do this?" but "How can I come to know God better in and through this?"

Not "Why is God allowing this struggle?" but "How can I grow in faith and trust in and through this struggle?"

Not "Why would God allow this setback?" but "How might we and the world around us see God's goodness and love in this situation?"

When we move from why to how, we begin to allow—to welcome, even—the transformation. As Carla McClafferty discovered as she processed the death of her toddler son, "Sometimes, God doesn't change our circumstances, He changes us in our circumstances."[7]

REALIZE THAT GOD IS GRIEVING TOO

As we continue to change the questions we ask in our pain, we not only allow ourselves chances to see God's goodness but discover something else: God is grieving too. Ann Voskamp describes this as she relates the story of Noah in *The Greatest Gift*. She points to the verse that reveals "[God's] heart was deeply troubled" (Genesis 6:6) and posits that our infinite God, who is everywhere present in this immeasurable universe, has—let's make that *is*—a love that encompasses everything. "God has a heart," Voskamp reminds us. "It hurts with what hurts us. His heart hurts not just with a few drops of ache, not just with a slow drip of sadness—the whole expanse of His heart fills, swells, weighs dark with this storm of pain."[8]

Why does God grieve? He does so vicariously on our behalf. Over the choices we've made. Over Adam and Eve's sin and every flawed day thereafter, in which He experiences His precious, impeccably created cosmos crumbling in its sin-broken state. He grieves for His own Son, who for us became radically disabled—His heavenly position relinquished and His divine prerogatives overridden as He willingly took upon Himself our dying humanity so that we, disfigured though we are by sin, could live in His presence in, through, and despite life's storms (see Philippians 2:6–7). Truly, as Voskamp concludes, "time only continues on in this impossibly suffering world because God Himself is willing to keep suffering the impossible with us."[9]

Every day we suffer, God weeps. Our
lives—our children's lives, and all the
challenges they bring—continue by
His tears, not His indifference.

Every day we suffer, God weeps. Our lives—our children's lives, and all the challenges they bring—continue by His tears, not His indifference. When we take the time to see God and even wrestle with Him, our grief somehow shrinks in the presence of His. And somehow, because God makes all things work toward a good end, at the same time our joy expands.

REFRAME THE MEMORIES

Speaking of God making all things work for the good . . . what exactly does that mean? I've read through the Bible quite a few times in my life, and I can't help but notice that people who live for God don't overwhelmingly have "good" lives.

Joseph, the favored son from among Jacob's twelve, no doubt didn't construe it as good to be thrown in a pit, sold into slavery, betrayed by his owner's wife, or forgotten in prison for years (see Genesis 37 and 39–45). I know that the apostle Paul, once a devout Jewish leader, didn't feel great about being blinded in the middle of the road on his way to accomplish what he thought God had called him to do (see Acts 9). And Jesus Himself endured a moment when God's plan scared Him so thoroughly that He sweat drops of blood, pleading with God to reveal a Plan B by which He could still accomplish the Father's will (Luke 22:42–44). In the short run, these figures found themselves in the thick of the fray, and their situations didn't feel as though they were heading in a positive direction. From the "here and now" perspective they seemed anything but good; they were undeniably miserable, painful experiences. But, as Max Lucado writes in his book *You'll Get Through This*, "In God's hands intended evil becomes eventual good."[10] In each case I mentioned, it's clear that this was true:

> Joseph was released from prison and went on to save an entire region from famine by the wisdom he'd gained in and through years of turmoil and time to think.
>
> Paul recovered his sight and took the insight God invested in him to evangelize an entire region with the good news about Jesus.
>
> Jesus rose from that blood-sweat ordeal of prayer, faced a mob, was

tortured and crucified, . . . and then arose again, thereby defeating sin, death, and their evil instigator for all time.

All things work together for good for those who love and serve the Lord. "Okay," you may be thinking, "but what possible good can come from my child's disability or my family's struggle?" Why don't *you tell me*. Or better yet, think this through and inform yourself. Consider the following questions for a few moments in the quiet of your heart:

What good has come so far from the challenges your child and/or your family has faced? I'm not suggesting that the diagnoses and difficulties were in any way good, but what else in your situation has been? I know that my own answer includes that I've had the opportunity to speak to thousands of moms, to encourage them and help them uncover their humor even in their darkest times. I was first invited to speak after adopting our older two girls because people at my church wanted to know how I managed to keep showing up when things were as hard as they were. The rest, as they say, is history. A history of people around the world encouraged, supported—hopefully even by reading this book—because of the challenges we've faced in our family.

What aspect of God's heart might you never have known if not for the loss you've experienced? What formerly childish ways of engaging life or the world have been replaced by maturity in the presence of loss and struggle? In my life, I'd have to say it's how I pray. As a college kid I offered up long, elaborate prayers. I'd literally spend hours asking God to work in the world. It wasn't until I faced our first loss in the context of family that I discovered that prayer is a two-way conversation. Not that I hear God speak to me aloud or anything like that, but prayer requires at least as much listening as speaking. We're in relationship with God, after all, so prayer shouldn't sound as though we're talking to a cosmic vending machine! If not for the deep grief we've been through in our family, I'd probably still be bossing God around in prayer, instead of sitting with Him, listening for His heart for people, and praying along those lines.

What about you? What's your story? How might you reframe what God's been up to in your life and family so far? As a coach, may I challenge you to come up with at least five answers? Stretch that brain. Let's see what joy God's been cultivating all around and within you, even in the hardest seasons.

LET JOY IN

This may seem like a no-brainer, but it's not. Once we've had life's circumstances go for our emotional jugular a few times, it's human nature to try to stanch the bleeding. As Brené Brown puts it in *Daring Greatly*, "It's easier to live disappointed than it is to feel disappointed. It feels more vulnerable to dip in and out of disappointment than to just set up camp there. You sacrifice joy, but you suffer less pain."[11] That is, it's easier to set our default position to joyless than it is to be vitally present in the present, truly open to possible joy moments, knowing even as we do that they can't possibly last forever. We won't get hurt as acutely if we live that way, we tell ourselves. It sets the expectation low, so we're not disappointed when God (or whoever else it is who's responsible!) throws a monkey wrench into our hopes.

You know what they say about low expectations, though, right? If you aim low or have minimal hopes for good, you'll hit your goal every time. As safe as that may seem at times to be, do we really want the black-and-white version of life when we could revel in the joy-tinted Technicolor one? It's true that grief hurts like crazy. Loving a child until their too-soon last breath almost breaks us. Listening to our middle schooler with mental health challenges as she berates the hard-won friend—her first ever—to the point the other girl says, "Maybe we just shouldn't be friends," rips right through a parent's heart. We can struggle with all the issues we've talked about in this book with all the people we know over time, and it can feel as though it's bleeding the life out of us. But fighting joy—holding it at arm's reach so we'll never be hurt or joyless again—isn't truly safe. It only ensures that we'll live with much less, both in terms of quality and quantity. And this stance only prolongs the pain we're trying to avoid.

Fighting joy—holding it at arm's
reach so we'll never be hurt or joyless
again—isn't truly safe. It only ensures
that we'll live with much less, both in
terms of quality and quantity.

As we're seeing God's heart, as well as our situation and His role in it, with fresh eyes, let's not set up camp in disappointment. Let's grasp God's outstretched hand, lean into Him, and take the risk to choose joy both in and in spite of all our convoluted circumstances. If not for ourselves, for the world around us. Because our struggles aren't just our stories—they're God's story. We live in community, on a planet full of equally struggling people. As Mary DeMuth has earlier reminded us, healing happens in community. Allowing God to cultivate joy in us as we face loss, setbacks, and stress becomes a way in which both we and the rest of the world come to know God's heart and help.

I saw this recently as I sat at an orthodontist appointment for my second daughter. We were about to have the braces, for which we'd paid dearly, removed six months before they accomplished what we paid for. During the year and a half our child was in the residential facility, the focus had been on getting her safe and able to live at home, in a family environment. That focus of practical necessity didn't include stellar dental hygiene when she couldn't manage her emotions and was wetting and soiling herself consistently. The braces had suffered for it, and we'd had to relent and give up on that round of orthodontia. But that didn't make me happy about it!

As I sat, frustrated over yet another area of collateral damage caused by our kids' special needs, I noticed a mom and daughter sitting across from us in the waiting room. They weren't more than five feet away, but I could see in this other mom's eyes that her thoughts were much further afield. I thought to myself, "She's hurting." I didn't have any particular reason to think that. She didn't look upset, just distant. But as a mom who's sat in myriad waiting rooms with my children, staring out windows while trying not to burst into tears of weariness, frustration, or grief, I recognized something familiar in her absent look. I found myself praying for her—not a well-worded wish-list prayer but groans of understanding, pleading for God's comfort that has so often surprised me in dark times. As I prayed silently for her, she turned and caught my eye. A tear glistened and spilled down her cheek. She turned back to look out the window, and my prayers swelled stronger. In that instant of contact she shared an ache with me, a stranger. Nobody else in the room seemed to notice her or her silent struggle. But I've been that mom. The one sitting woodenly in a room while far from actively present. The one whose mind is light years away, riddled with anxiety, discouragement, and grief.

I reached into my purse, pulled out a pack of tissues, and offered them across the wide silence between us. Her smile—broken, beautiful—brought tears to my eyes. In a single moment, without effort, without sharing life stories, I felt God's powerful presence. He became real to me as I noticed and extended a tissue to another hurting mom. A simple act, but a tangible reminder of the truth that God "comforts us in all our troubles, so that we can comfort those in any trouble with the comfort we ourselves receive from God" (2 Corinthians 1:4).

God doesn't initiate our pain, our children's diagnoses, or our impossibly complicated therapeutic schedules. He doesn't bring about the broken relationships that result as we try to navigate through friendships, extended family relationships, community involvement, and interactions at school and in doctors' offices. He doesn't wish for us or for our kids to suffer. But, as Max Lucado encourages, "[We'll] get through this. It won't be painless. It won't be quick. But God will use this mess for good."[12] God takes what life and sin intended for evil, reweaving it into a tapestry that becomes the comfort others wrap around their weary shoulders too.

That truth yields joy we can grab on to, friends. Grab on to and never, ever, let go.

NEXT STEPS

You've read through this book and made choices to spend your time here for a brief season. The enemy would love to see the insights and healing that's begun here become a distant, ineffective memory. Don't let that happen! Take a stand and make the choice today to keep moving forward. Wherever you are in your journey, will you take at least one of these steps today? Consider these questions:

What idea(s) most challenged me in this book?
What is the next joy-building step I need to take?
What will I need in order to make that happen? (Create some goals.)

Connect with a friend or your pastor to let him or her know what you're learning and where you feel God leading you next.

Subscribe to receive my weekly supportive blog posts delivered free to your inbox, and receive a free e-book with practical joy-building tips when you do (LaurieWallin.com).

Join the community at www.facebook.com/LivingPowerLifeCoaching, where you'll receive inspiration, quotations, and questions that invite joy through the week.

Email me at LaurieWallin@LaurieWallin.com to set up your free thirty-minute coaching session and start moving toward confident, joy-filled living as a parent.

I'd love to help you step fully into who God designed you uniquely to be. As a coach, I've helped clients worldwide save time, energy, and frustration by (re)discovering their strengths and passions, regaining health and balance, and pursuing dreams. I'd be honored to support you in pressing into all God has for you and your family too.

With love and admiration for all you do,

Laurie

NOTES

CHAPTER 1: YES, YOU *CAN* ENJOY LIFE AGAIN

1. *National Geographic: Stress: Portrait of a Killer* (Washington, DC: National Geographic Video, 2008), DVD.
2. Victoria Secunda, *When Madness Comes Home* (New York: Hyperion, 1998), 2.
3. Anne Lamott, *Traveling Mercies: Some Thoughts on Faith* (New York: Anchor Books, 1999), 134.
4. Asa Brown, "Forgiveness," Canadian Counseling and Psychotherapy Association blog, April 15, 2013, http://www.ccpa-accp.ca/blog /?p=2820.

CHAPTER 2: LOOKING IN THE MIRROR

1. Gillian Marchenko, "Can't Take Much More of My Child with Special Needs," blog, August 29, 2012, http://www.gillianmarchenko .com/cant-take-much-more-of-my-child-with-special-needs/.
2. Ethan Kross, Philippe Verduyn, Emre Demiralp, Jiyoung Park, David Seungjae Lee, et. al, "Facebook Use Predicts Declines in Subjective Well-Being in Young Adults," *PLoS ONE* 8, no. 8 (August 14, 2013): e69841, doi: 10.1371/journal.pone.0069841.
3. Hui-Tzu Grace Chou and Nicholas Edge, "They Are Happier and Having Better Lives Than I Am": The Impact of Using Facebook on Perceptions of Others' Lives, *Cyberpsychology, Behavior, and Social Networking* 15, no. 2 (February 9, 2012): 117–21, doi: 10.1089 /cyber.2011.0324.

4. Gillian Marchenko, *Sun Shine Down: A Memoir* (New York: T.S. Poetry Press, 2013), 85–86.

5. Marlena Graves, "Getting to the Root of Female Masturbation," *Christianity Today*, her•meneutics, January 5, 2012, http://www .christianitytoday.com/women/2012/january/getting-to-root-of -female-masturbation.html.

6. Mark Twain, "Which Was the Dream?" *Mark Twain's "Which Was the Dream?" and Other Symbolic Writings of the Later Years*, edited by John S. Tuckey (Berkeley: University of California Press, 1968), 45.

7. Everett L. Worthington Jr., "Dealing With Self-Condemnation Through Responsible Self-Forgiveness," *Christian Counseling Connection* 19, no. 3 (2013), 12.

8. (in)Able: moms of kids with special needs, An (in)Courage community, https://www.facebook.com/groups/inablespecialneeds/322991 831191613/.

CHAPTER 3: RESTORING JOY IN HOW YOU SEE YOURSELF

1. Julie Ann Barnhill, *Scandalous Grace: Celebrate the Liberating and Tantalizing Realities of Divine Grace* (Wheaton, IL: Tyndale, 2004), 91.

2. Holley Gerth, *You're Already Amazing: Embracing Who You Are, Becoming All God Created You To Be* (Grand Rapids: Revell, 2012), 23; italics mine.

3. John Eldredge, *Waking the Dead: The Glory of a Heart Fully Alive* (Nashville: Thomas Nelson, 2003), 88.

4. Holley Gerth, *You're Made for a God-Sized Dream: Opening the Door to All God Has for You* (Grand Rapids: Revell, 2013), 25.

5. Margie M., phone interview, November 8, 2013.

6. The Free Dictionary, s.v. "grace," accessed November 16, 2013, http://www.thefreedictionary.com/grace.

7. J. Hampton Keathley, "Grace and Peace," Bible.org, April 22, 2005, https://bible.org/article/grace-and-peace.

CHAPTER 4: WHEN SPECIAL NEEDS DON'T FEEL SPECIAL

1. Suzanne Eller, *The Unburdened Heart: Finding the Freedom of Forgiveness* (Grand Rapids: Regal, 2013), 99.

CHAPTER 5: REDISCOVERING JOY WITH YOUR SPECIAL CHILD

1. Melody Beattie, *Beyond Codependency* (Center City, MN: Hazelden Foundation, 1989), 18.
2. Mary Sheedy Kurcinka, *Raising Your Spirited Child Workbook* (New York: HarperCollins, 1998), 2.
3. Ibid.
4. Ibid., 21.
5. John W. James and Russell Friedman, *The Grief Recovery Handbook*, 20th Anniversary Expanded Edition (New York: Harper Collins, 2009), 3.
6. Ibid., 32.
7. Terri Mauro, "Acceptance and Forgiveness Are Not the Same as Weakness," About.com, Children with Special Needs, July 31, 2008, http://specialchildren.about.com/b/2008/07/30/acceptance-and -forgiveness-are-not-the-same-as-weakness.htm. Blog was discontinued in spring of 2014 and this web address is no longer active.

CHAPTER 6: FOR BETTER OR FOR WORSE

1. "Compassion Fatigue: An Expert Interview with Charles R. Figley, MS, PhD," *Medscape*, October 17, 2005, http://www.medscape.com/ viewarticle/513615.
2. Elisa Morgan, *The Beauty of Broken: My Story and Likely Yours Too* (Nashville: Thomas Nelson, 2013), 14.
3. Mary DeMuth, *The Wall Around Your Heart: How Jesus Heals You When Others Hurt You* (Nashville: Thomas Nelson, 2013), 24.
4. "Marriage Vows. Christianity: Anglican," Wikipedia.org, accessed November 19, 2013. http://en.wikipedia.org/wiki/Marriage_vows.
5. "The Charters of Freedom: The Declaration of Independence," United States Government Archives, accessed November 19, 2013, http://www.archives.gov/exhibits/charters/declaration_transcript .html.
6. "Table 1336. Marriage and Divorce Rates by Country: 1980 to 2008," *U.S. Census Bureau, Statistical Abstract of the United States: 2012*, http://www.census.gov/compendia/.

7. "Depression Around the World: How Do Countries Stack Up?" *Huffington Post*, July 27, 2011, http://www.huffingtonpost.com/2011/07 /27/depressed-countries_n_910345.html#s316418title=France_21.

8. Cindi McMenamin, *When a Woman Overcomes Life's Hurts* (Eugene, OR: Harvest House, 2012), 115.

9. Definition of *sozo*, Greek word for "to save . . . preserve . . . deliver." *Strong's Concordance* number 4982, BibleStudyTools.com, accessed November 19, 2013, http://www.biblestudytools.com/lexicons/greek /nas/sozo.html.

10. McMenamin, *When a Woman Overcomes Life's Hurts*, 118.

11. Greg Lucas, "This Is My Son," Not Alone blog, October 8, 2013, http://specialneedsparenting.net/son-autism/.

CHAPTER 7: REKINDLING JOY WITH YOUR SPOUSE

1. John Eldredge, *Waking the Dead: The Glory of a Heart Fully Alive* (Nashville: Thomas Nelson, 2003), 14.

2. Hartley Steiner, "Marriage Advice Moms Don't Want To Hear: It Isn't Your Husband's Fault," Hartley's Life with 3 Boys, January 2011, http://hartleysboys.blogspot.com/2011/01/marriage-advice-moms -dont-want-to-hear.html.

3. Ibid.

4. Elizabeth Gilbert, *Committed: A Skeptic Makes Peace with Marriage* (New York: Viking, 2010), 214.

5. Anne Dohrenwend, "Serving Up the Feedback Sandwich," *Family Practice Management* 9, no. 10 (Nov–Dec 2002), 43–46, http://www .aafp.org/fpm/2002/1100/p43.html.

6. Laura E. Marshak and Fran Pollock Prezant, *Married with Special-Needs Children: A Couples' Guide to Keeping Connected* (Bethesda, MD: Woodbine House, 2007), xiii.

7. Michael Fulwiler, "The Research: Predicting Divorce Among Newlyweds from the First Three Minutes of a Marital Conflict Discussion," The Gottman Institute Relationship blog, March 13, 2013, http://www.gottmanblog.com/2013/03/the-research-predicting -divorce-among.html.

8. Ellie Lisitsa, "The Positive Perspective: Dr. Gottman's Magic Ratio!,"

The Gottman Institute Relationship blog, December 5, 2012, http://www.gottmanblog.com/2012/12/the-positive-perspective-dr-gottmans.html.

9. Ellie Lisitsa, "The Sound Relationship House: The Positive Perspective," The Gottman Institute Relationship blog, November 28, 2012, http://www.gottmanblog.com/2012/11/the-sound-relationship-house-positive.html.

CHAPTER 8: CAN'T WE ALL JUST GET ALONG?

1. Lena, "The Lonely, Lonely World," blog, October 21, 2010, http://grherrin.livejournal.com/6305.html.
2. Jim Butcher, *Proven Guilty*, The Dresden Files series (New York: Roc, 2006), 291.
3. Marjorie Pay Hinckley, *Glimpses into the Life and Heart of Marjorie Pay Hinckley* (Salt Lake City: Deseret Book, 1999), 60.

CHAPTER 9: REGAINING JOY IN YOUR FAMILY

1. Hara Estroff Marano, "Our Brain's Negative Bias," *Psychology Today*, June 20, 2003, http://www.psychologytoday.com/articles/200306/our-brains-negative-bias.
2. June Hunt. *Rejection: Healing a Wounded Heart* (Torrance, CA: Aspire Press, 2013), 19.
3. Linda Breitman, *The Real You: Believing Your True Identity* (San Diego, CA: Linda Breitman Ministries, 2013), 31.
4. Ibid., 64.
5. Suzanne Eller, "*The Unburdened Heart* study week #5—I move from the past to the present," March 26, 2013, Suzanne Eller: Leading Women in a New Direction blog, http://tsuzanneeller.com/2013/03/26/the-unburdened-heart-study-week-5-i-move-from-the-past-to-the-present/.
6. Ibid.

CHAPTER 10: WHEN THE PROS DON'T KNOW

1. Suzanne Eller, *The Unburdened Heart: Finding the Freedom of Forgiveness* (Grand Rapids: Regal, 2013), 77.

CHAPTER 11: RECLAIMING JOY AND CONFIDENCE WITH THE PROS

1. Barbara Dittrich, "The Dirty Job of Special Needs Parenting," Not Alone blog, February 19, 2013, http://specialneedsparenting.net /the-dirty-job-of-special-needs-parenting/.
2. Jennifer Johnson, "Creating a Special Needs Binder," The Thinking Person's Guide to Autism, September 16, 2010, http://www.thinking autismguide.com/2010/09/creating-special-needs-binder.html. Used by permission.
3. Jolene Philo, *The Caregiver's Notebook: An Organizational Tool and Support to Help You Care for Others* (Grand Rapids: Discovery House). Scheduled for release in 2014.
4. Jolene Philo, *Different Dream Parenting* (Grand Rapids: Discovery House, 2011).
5. Carrie Fancett Pagels, "Stigmatized Kids: Learning and Intellectual Disabilities." *Christian Counseling Today* 20, no. 2 (2013): 26.
6. "WMA Declaration of Geneva," World Medical Association, accessed February 24, 2014, http://www.wma.net/en/30publications /10policies/g1/.
7. Jon Acuff, "10 Words That Erase Most Online Hate," October 29, 2013, http://acuff.me/2013/10/10-words-erase-online-hate/.
8. Brené Brown, *Daring Greatly: How the Courage to Be Vulnerable Transforms the Way We Live, Love, Parent, and Lead* (New York: Gotham Books, 2012), 124.

CHAPTER 12: LIFE ON THE SIDELINES

1. Emily Colson, "Is Your Church Open to Autism?" *Christianity Today*, January 10, 2011, http://www.christianitytoday.com/women /2011/january/is-your-church-open-to-autism.html.
2. Jackie Mills-Fernald and Jim Pierson, *Special Families . . . A Casserole's Not Enough*, (McLean, VA: McLean Bible Church Access Ministry, n.d.), 5, accessed December 6, 2013, http://www.mbctysons .org/uploads/ACC-SpecialFamily-Booklet-web.pdf.
3. Lucille Zimmerman, *Renewed: Finding Your Inner Happy in an Overwhelmed World* (Nashville: Abingdon, 2013), 131.
4. Ibid., 134.

5. Heather McFarland, August 29, 2012 (6:56 p.m.), comment on "Can't Take Much More of My Child With Special Needs," Gillian Marchenko, August 29, 2012, http://www.gillianmarchenko.com /cant-take-much-more-of-my-child-with-special-needs/.
6. Mills-Fernald and Pierson, *Special Families . . . A Casserole's Not Enough*, 11.
7. Zimmerman, *Renewed*, 163.

CHAPTER 13: REBUILDING JOY IN COMMUNITY

1. Tom Rath and Jim Harter, *Wellbeing: The Five Essential Elements* (New York: Gallup Press, 2010), 37.
2. Dictionary.com, s.v. "mindfulness," accessed November 30, 2013, http://dictionary.reference.com/browse/mindfulness?s=t.
3. Mark Myers, "Mindfulness and the Brain: How to Change Your Life," *Christian Counseling Today* 20, no. 3 (2013), 63.
4. Megan Goates, "I Used to Be a Perfect Mom, but My Special-Needs Kids Taught Me Otherwise," KSL.com, September 17, 2013, http:// www.ksl.com/?sid=26799174.
5. Kaci Calvaresi, August 29, 2012 (7:42 p.m.), comment on "Can't Take Much More of My Child With Special Needs" Gillian Marchenko, August 29, 2012, http://www.gillianmarchenko.com/cant -take-much-more-of-my-child-with-special-needs/.
6. Kathryn Sneed, "Blessings in Disguise," April 11, 2013, Not Alone blog, http://specialneedsparenting.net/blessings-in-disguise/.

CHAPTER 14: IS GOD EVEN LISTENING?

1. Carla Killough McClafferty, *Forgiving God: A Woman's Struggle to Understand When God Answers No* (Grand Rapids: Discovery House, 1995), 58.
2. Laurie Wallin, *Why Your Weirdness Is Wonderful: Embrace Your Quirks and Live Your Strengths* (Nashville, Abingdon, 2014), 17.
3. McClafferty, *Forgiving God*, 79.
4. John Bevere, "John Bevere: What Is the Glory of the Lord?" Charisma Magazine.com, June 4, 2013, http://www.charismamag.com/spirit /supernatural/17927-john-bevere-what-is-the-glory-of-the-lord.
5. Ibid.

CHAPTER 15: REDISCOVERING JOY WITH GOD

1. I searched for each of those words—*joy, forgiveness, salvation,* and *grace*—in the King James Version on HolyBible.com.
2. This concept of earning our own joy is taught in Buddhism. See Eknath Easwaran, *The Dhammapada,* large print edition (Tomales, CA: Nilgiri Press, 2007), xli.
3. Charles Spurgeon, "The Joy of the Lord, the Strength of His People" (sermon no. 1027, Metropolitan Tabernacle, London, December 31, 1871), http://www.spurgeon.org/sermons/1027.htm.
4. Mary DeMuth, *The Wall Around Your Heart: How Jesus Heals You When Others Hurt You* (Nashville: Thomas Nelson, 2013), 52.
5. Ann Voskamp, *One Thousand Gifts: A Dare to Live Fully Right Where You Are* (Grand Rapids: Zondervan, 2010), 16.
6. Lucille Zimmerman, *Renewed: Finding Your Inner Happy in an Overwhelmed World* (Nashville: Abingdon, 2013), 178.
7. Carla Killough McClafferty, *Forgiving God: A Woman's Struggle to Understand When God Answers No* (Grand Rapids: Discovery House, 1995), 106.
8. Ann Voskamp, *The Greatest Gift: Unwrapping the Full Love Story of Christmas* (Carol Stream, IL: Tyndale House, 2013), 30.
9. Ibid.
10. Max Lucado, *You'll Get Through This: Hope and Help for Your Turbulent Times* (Nashville: Thomas Nelson, 2013), 7.
11. Brené Brown, *Daring Greatly: How the Courage to Be Vulnerable Transforms the Way We Live, Love, Parent, and Lead* (New York: Gotham Books, 2012), 120.
12. Lucado, *You'll Get Through This,* 3.

ABOUT THE AUTHOR

Laurie Wallin is a Christian speaker and certified life coach. Over the past several years, she's helped parents worldwide regain joy and confidence in their special families by letting go of energy drainers and using their God-inspired strengths. Laurie writes regularly for her own site, LaurieWallin.com, contributing to SpecialHappens.com, SpecialNeedsParenting.net, GodSizedDreams.com, and the Women of Faith blog as well. She's also the author of *Why Your Weirdness Is Wonderful* (Abingdon Press, 2014), a book designed to help all of us—parents of special needs or not—discover the goodness and strength God's built into the quirks we fight so hard in ourselves.

Laurie, her husband, and their four daughters make their home in San Diego.